STAMFORD
PAST

An aerial view of Stamford from the south-west.

STAMFORD PAST

Christopher Davies

Phillimore

2002

Published by
PHILLIMORE & CO. LTD
Shopwyke Manor Barn, Chichester, West Sussex

ISBN 1 86077 228 5

Printed and bound in Great Britain by
BIDDLES LTD
Guildford, Surrey

Contents

List of Illustrations

Frontispiece: Aerial view of Stamford

Acknowledgements

The author wishes to thank the following for permission to reproduce illustrations. Stamford Town Council for the cover picture; *Peterborough Evening Telegraph* for the frontispiece; Stamford Museum, 9; Martin Smith 16,19; Stamford Local History Society, 21, 46; Lady Victoria Leatham, 35; Mr C. Bennett, 133; The Stamford Survey Group, 5-6, 11, 14, 20, 30, 31, 40, 41, 43, 44 49, 50, 52-4, 57, 59, 61, 62, 66-68, 70, 76, 80, 81, 84-6, 91-3, 95-7, 100, 101, 104-6, 108, 110, 111-120, 122, 126, 130-2, 134-6. All other photographs are from the author's own collection.

Thanks are also due to Michael Thompson for his helpful comments on the early chapters and to Daniel Lezano for his help with the cover photograph; to Tracey Crawley and the staff of Stamford Museum; and to the staff of Stamford Library, Leicester University Library and the staff of Lincolnshire and Northamptonshire Record Offices.

Introduction

The story of Stamford's historical development has been told many times. It is difficult therefore, in re-telling this story not to be derivative of the many excellent works that have preceded it. I have opted therefore for a broad brush approach and sought to answer specific questions about the town. In particular, how an Anglo-Danish borough became the Georgian town '*par excellence*'; and how that Georgian town became a dormitory of nearby Peterborough.

Stamford has always attracted superlatives. As long ago as 1697, Celia Fiennes described the town 'as fine a built town all of stone as may be seen'. Praise for the town has been unabated ever since. That the town has been come down to us relatively unchanged is due, in part, to the lack of 19th-century industrialisation, but also to the delay in enclosing the open fields to the north of the town. Stamford's town centre has not suffered redevelopment in the way that Peterborough or Grantham have. The unique nature of the town was recognised in 1967 when it was designated the first Conservation Area in the country.

Professor Alan Rogers, writing in *The Book of Stamford*, describes the town's history as one of missed opportunities. There is more than a little truth in this, but, with the benefit of hindsight, we should perhaps be grateful that some of these missed opportunities have helped to preserve the town as it is today. But towns change to reflect the age, and the people living in them. Therein lies Stamford's current problem: how to preserve the architectural integrity of the town and still meet the needs of the 21st century. Year by year a little more of the town's history is destroyed by replacement, alteration or poor design. Preservation of the historic core of the town is an issue of some importance, particularly if the future lies in developing tourism.

Economically, Stamford faces an uncertain future, particularly when so many decisions that affect the town are taken remotely in Grantham. The early years of the new millennium have seen a number of long established local companies close. This has forced more and more people to look outside of the town for their livelihood. Paradoxically, as more people recognise the town as a pleasant place in which to live, the town's population is growing. This has resulted in an unprecedented level of building, many former commercial sites being turned over to housing. It is difficult to say where the town's future lies. One thing is certain: history has shown that, faced with difficult circumstances, Stamford will eventually overcome them.

CHRISTOPHER DAVIES

One

The Danish Burh and Anglo-Saxon Settlement

WE CAN POINT to two major factors that influenced settlement in the area that became Stamford. Firstly, the natural bounty of the Welland valley provided most of what the settlers would need. An ample supply of water from the river and the many wells in the area, together with good grazing land, fertile soil and a plentiful supply of timber made this an ideal place in which to settle.

Just as significant was the fact that emerging Stamford lay on what we now call the Jurassic way, that prehistoric track route which followed the limestone belt across England from Dorset, through the Midlands to the Humber. A crossing at this point was no accident, since this was one of the few places locally where the Welland could easily be forded for most of the year, the flood-plain widening significantly on either side of the present town. The Roman Ermine Street ran locally between the two encampments of Durobrivae in the south and Great Casterton to the north. It crossed the Welland half a mile upstream from the narrowest point of the flood-plain, at a point where easy gradients of the valley sides create a good crossing place. The line of Ermine Street is still defined by the modern Water Furlong and Roman Bank.

Other reasons apart, Stamford came into being at a place where the river Welland could easily be forded. The name Stamford is derived from Stony Ford or Stone Ford. By the 10th century it had become Steanford, although Staunford was also used. Stanford was in common use by 1086, and this gradually became Stamford.

Ermine Street, the forerunner of the modern A1, was an important route for the Romans. It linked London with the fortresses at Lincoln and beyond, marked the line taken by the advancing Ninth Legion soon after A.D. 43, and established their main road from London to York. It is possible, therefore, that the hutments of Roman outposts guarding the ford were the beginnings of the town of Stamford.

The principal Roman settlement near Stamford was at Great Casterton, and it is possible that this site was occupied by the Saxons until the sixth century. The pattern of Anglo-Saxon settlement in the Stamford area can be determined by place names. To the south of the Welland, on a ridge overlooking the valley, there is a series of villages and village sites. These lie from one to two miles apart and include Collyweston, Easton, Wothorpe, Burghley, Pilsgate and Barnack. To the north, and much closer to the river, we find Ketton, Tinwell, Uffington, Tallington and West Deeping. Stamford would clearly fit into this pattern between Tinwell and Uffington.

On this evidence alone it would be reasonable to suspect a settlement on the Stamford site. To some extent, this can be supported by the discovery of a section of defensive ditch

1

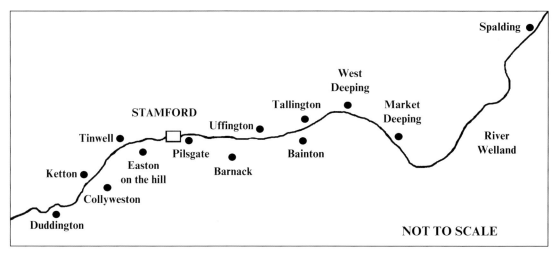

Spalding ●

West
Deeping

Tallington

STAMFORD   Market
                      Deeping
Uffington ●

Tinwell ●   River
           □   Pilsgate ●   Welland
                                    Bainton ●
Easton   Barnack ●
on the hill

Ketton ●

Collyweston

Duddington   **NOT TO SCALE**

1 Map showing the village sites around the Stamford area.

during the excavations of the castle site in the 1970s. This may have related to a late ninth-century enclosure and it has been conjectured that these ditches might have protected an early fortified house. The castle was situated in the St Peter's area of Stamford which, at that time, belonged to the ancient Mercian royal estate of *Roteland* or Rutland. Certainly, from the 10th century, perhaps even earlier, this estate had formed part of the dowry of the Mercian queens and was endowed with an area of land that lay to the west of Ermine Street.

This area which, after the Conquest, became known as Portland, appears to have been well sited. It stood on a defensible hill just above the route to the early river crossing. This route may have run down the modern Wothorpe Road, across the meadows and up a stream valley which later became Castle Dyke. The case for this being an Anglo-Saxon settlement is further supported by the location of St Peter's Church. A church was often built next to an enclosure to serve the religious needs of the lord. It is quite possible, therefore, that St Peter's, which stood nearby, served this purpose.

The Danes migrated into the East Midlands and were not slow to recognise the advantages of settlement in this area. In 877 they established

a borough to the east of the earlier enclosure on terraces to the north of the narrowest point in the river valley. Evidence for this early borough exists today in the street layout. The present High Street formed the main axial road, with the modern St John's Street and Star Lane indicating its eastern and western extent.

Places like Stamford were not just centres for the garrison of soldiers, but evolving communities of Danish and Saxon people sustained by agriculture and industry. Stamford, in common with York, Lincoln, Norwich and Thetford, experienced a significant growth in economic activity. This was aided by Viking supremacy on the seas which enabled trading links with the Baltic countries and Russia. Evidence from Domesday Book suggests that eastern England, under Danish influence, was wealthier and more heavily populated than the rest of the country.

At Stamford the area between the two areas of early settlement, which we now know as Red Lion Square and Sheepmarket, developed into an important market place for the trading of produce both from the town's growing industries and crafts, including widespread iron smelting in the east, and from the agricultural land that surrounded the town. An important industry to emerge at this time was that of ceramics. The Danes brought with them potters experienced in the production of wheel-thrown pottery, a type unknown in England since the departure of the Romans. The availability of good local clays elevated Stamford into a major pottery centre. Although production concentrated on cheap cooking pots for local use, there was also a more prestigious range which has come to be known as Stamford ware, which found its way all over Britain and the Continent by means of Viking trading routes.

Development of this early pottery, which appeared about a hundred years after the Norman Conquest, became known as Stamford ware. This was characterised by being decorated with a lead glaze. There was considerable variation in the colour of these glazes but blue, green, yellow and orange are the most common. Excavations in the town during the 19th and 20th centuries have uncovered kilns around the edges of the early settlements, at the castle site and at St Paul's Street. Not only do these indicate extensive industry at the time, but also the sphere of Danish influence.

The Danes, as the result of a treaty with King Alfred in 878, were restricted to an area we now call the Danelaw, roughly the eastern and northern half of England. Stamford was within the area of the Danelaw, and it was in these areas that Danish legal and social

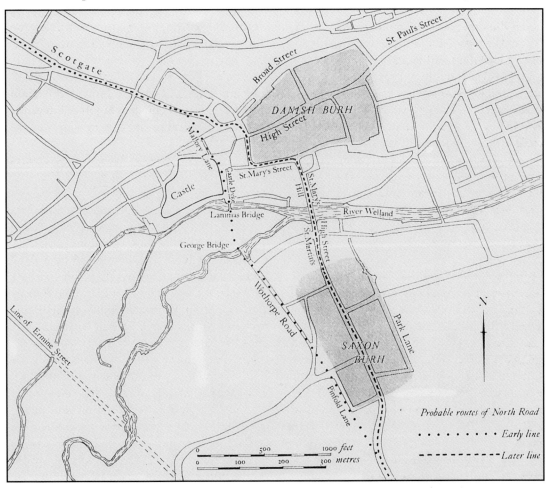

2 Map showing the area of the Danish Burh (877) and the Saxon Burh (918).

customs prevailed from the late ninth century until the Norman Conquest. From the Anglo-Saxon Chronicle we learn that Stamford, along with Leicester, Lincoln, Nottingham and Derby, was one of the five Danish Boroughs. These five were the controlling boroughs of the Danelaw and each centre had its own court, administration and legal identity as well as providing a base for one of the five Viking armies.

During the reigns of Alfred's son, Edward the Elder and his heir, Athelstan, there was a systematic reconquest of the Danelaw. The campaign was led by Edward himself and his sister Aethelflaed, 'Lady of the Mercians', who was determined to avenge the Danish raids made into Mercia in 913. Edward consolidated his position south of Stamford and, by 917, all the

Danish armies south of the Welland had submitted to him. At the same time Aethelflaed had kept the Danes busy in the Midlands and had gained control of Derby and Leicester.

It was during Edward's campaign that the Danish borough of Stamford was called upon to defend itself for the first time. In 918 the Anglo-Saxon Chronicle records that: 'In this year, between Rogation days and midsummer, king Edward marched with his levies to Stamford, and had a fortress built on the south bank of the river: all the people who owed allegiance to the more northerly fortress submitted to him and sought him for their lord and protector.'

The purpose of Edward's fortress was to control the crossing of one of the most important rivers in eastern England; a similar strategy

3 Late medieval houses in St Paul's Street.

to that which he had employed on the Ouse at Bedford and the Trent at Nottingham.

Edward's settlement was almost certainly on the site of the modern St Martin's area. From the topographical evidence we can conjecture that the settlement was sited above the flood plain, with the present High Street, St Martin's forming its axis. It was probably bounded on the east by Park Lane and on the west by Pinfold Lane. It seems likely that a bridge linking the two settlements was built shortly after the southern settlement was established and that this gave rise to a new route across the river, superseding the earlier one to the west. That the boundaries of the Danish borough were firmly established by this time is evidenced by the contorted route the new road took to skirt its southern and western edges, that is, along the modern St Mary's and St John's streets.

The death of Aethelflaed in 918 took Edward to the Mercian centre at Tamworth to secure the sovereignty of Wessex. From there he pressed north, taking Nottingham and establishing himself as the most powerful ruler in Britain. By 927 his son Athelstan had extended Wessex influence as far north as Penrith. Despite this, Danish allegiances remained. When Athelstan died in 939, a Norwegian army from Ireland, led by Olaf Guthfrithson, swept through the Midlands, encountering little resistance. Stamford came under his control, probably from the base he established at Leicester. However, the death of Olaf in 941 allowed King Edmund, brother and successor of Athelstan, to recover the lost territory quite quickly.

It is shortly after these events that the Anglo-Saxon Chronicle first mentions the military confederacy of the five boroughs of the Danelaw of which, as we have seen, Stamford was one. Although each centre had its own court, administration and legal identity, they were still subordinate to the ealdorman; this Anglo-Saxon royal official governed a shire or, during the 10th century, a group of shires.

Stamford and Lincoln also had a number of lawmen who were probably suitors to the court of the ealdorman.

Stamford's status at this time was confirmation of its national importance both strategically and economically. It had responsibility for a large administrative area to the north and east which covered the area of the present-day Kesteven and Holland. Its borough status also led to the foundation of a mint in about 940.

This early impetus to Stamford's growth suffered a set back during the reigns of Edgar (957-975) and Aethelred 'the Unready' (975-1016). The town failed to become a county town and its administrative lands were lost. The reasons for this were both political and geographical. The focus of national politics shifted north to the Humber area, and Stamford's military significance declined as a result. As was often to be the case in later years, Stamford was left out on a limb, hemmed in by Northamptonshire's territory to the south and the estate of Rutland to the west. To the east were the monasteries of Peterborough (refounded in 966) and Thorney (refounded in 972) as well as newer monasteries such as Ramsey which was founded about 969. These new, richly endowed houses were quick to compete for land and the area of Stamford south of the river soon came under the control of Peterborough Abbey.

The new 'shire' system of civil and military administration devised by the Wessex monarchy endorsed these changes. All the boroughs of the Danelaw, with the exception of Stamford, became county towns. By 1016, when Lincolnshire is first recorded, Stamford's military and administrative functions and dependent land had already passed to Lincoln. Stamford retained some shire-town functions and privileges throughout the Middle Ages, but the shire system has proved so efficient and enduring that Stamford now suffers from an anomalous and isolated position at the junction of four counties.

The reign of Aethelred saw the collapse of the Wessex empire. In 1002, Viking attacks into the Danelaw intensified and Aethelred, under considerable pressure, ordered that all Danes living in England should be massacred. This extraordinary command must have created chaos in areas of heavy Danish settlement such as Stamford, and prompted King Swein of Denmark to attack the following year. However, it took until 1013 for Swein to achieve success. Arriving via the Humber, he established a base at Gainsborough and marched south with his army. The five-borough confederacy collapsed and the people of the east midlands recognised him as their king. By the time Aethelred died in 1016, Swein was accepted as the king of England and, under the rule of his son Cnut, England effectively became part of the Danish empire. On Cnut's death the people of the East Midlands supported the succession of his son Harold Harefoot and afterwards Hardicnut.

On the eve of the Norman invasion, which was to change the face of Britain, Stamford was one of the largest and most prosperous towns in the country. It was heavily populated, industrialised, defended and a centre of trade with good inland communications and river transport to the Wash. However, Stamford's failure to become a county town was a crucial factor which was to have far-reaching consequences for the future.

Two

NORMAN INFLUENCES

THE NORMAN CONQUEST was an event of immense political, economic and social significance, which marked the end of Saxon England and the beginning of what we now call the Middle Ages. For many 1066 did not mark a dramatic break with what had gone before and their way of life remained largely unaltered, at least to begin with. However, between 1067 and 1070 there was a series of uprisings against Norman rule in various parts of the country, including the Midlands and East Anglia. Hereward the Wake is traditionally credited with leading the rising in the fenland area, but there appears to be no firm evidence to support this, nor for his ownership of nearby Bourne.

Clearly, William needed to move swiftly to put down these risings and to stamp Norman authority on the country. This done, and with all major resistance crushed, William began to set up castles to guard all towns and important junctions, so that future rebellions could be contained before they gathered momentum. A chronicler of the time wrote that the new King's fortifications were 'erected against the fickleness of the huge and fierce population'. Stamford's position on an important thoroughfare and river crossing, together with its close proximity to the troublesome events at Peterborough and the surrounding area, made it a prime candidate for fortification. Thus emerged a new phase in Stamford's military history with the establishment of a castle. The most likely date for the building of this castle would appear to be the early part of 1068 when

William took his first campaign into Lincoln-shire. It is interesting that Stamford is the only non-county town in which he chose to establish a castle.

The chosen site was that of the earlier fortified enclosure, next to St Peter's Church, presenting the most defensible position over-looking, as it did, the road and river crossing. We know from the Domesday Survey that five messuages were destroyed to make way for the castle. This was a simple motte and bailey structure to which, in later years, a circular keep was added. This was destroyed in the 1930s with, unfortunately, little record other than the bare fact that it enclosed an area 20 metres (65 ft) across. The bailey was excavated in 1971 before a modern housing development was built on the site.

Whilst the castle would have acted as a garrison point and a place of refuge in troubled times, it was not long before the town itself had some form of defence. The area of Stamford north of the Welland was probably walled by the 1180s, although it may be assumed that there were walls in some form in place as early as 1150. This assumption is based on the fact that in 1153 it took the Count of Anjou three assaults to capture the town. What these defences were in their early stage is not clear; they were probably of earth and wood, as they were often rebuilt. During the Barons' War grants were given for rebuilding the walls and in their final form they were of stone, thickly built and with sentry-walks along the top. There was a number

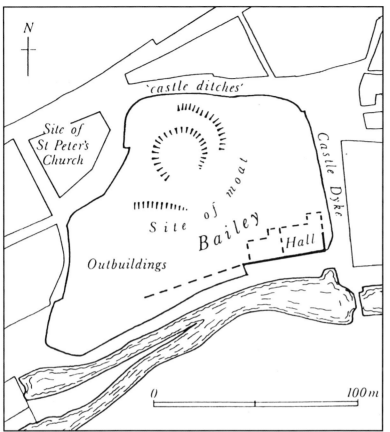

4 Map showing the site of the post-Conquest castle.

5 Stamford Castle: remains of the 12th-century keep, photographed during its demolition in 1933.

6 All that now remains of the castle is the east wall of the hall, which dates from the 13th century. The three doorways are probably service doorways to the lower end of the hall.

of round bastions built into the wall, a much mutilated example of which remains in West Street. Strong gate houses were built at each entrance to the town. St Martin's, of course, lay outside the town walls on the south bank of the Welland and quite early on came under the control of the Abbot of Peterborough. At this early stage in the town's history, and for many years after, there appears to have been some doubt as to whether St Martin's should properly be deemed part of Stamford.

Some twenty years after the Conquest the King's Commissioners were to record Stamford as part of the Domesday Survey. So what sort of town did they find? During its occupation by the Danes, Stamford had enjoyed a position of some importance and in the years of Saxon rule and beyond this importance was consolidated. This is reflected in the fact that from 979 until the 12th century a mint was functioning in the town. The large number of moneyers and of dies in use points to an out-

put exceeded only be larger towns such as London, Winchester, York and Lincoln. Although in *The Making of Stamford* Alan Rogers suggests that by 1086 Stamford may well have been less important than it had been a hundred years earlier, the town was indisputably still one of substance. It was listed as a royal borough (Stanford Burgum Regis) which signified that it had no overlord other than the king. Some 412 messuages are referred to in the five wards north of the river. The sixth ward, St Martin's, is not mentioned since that area of the town was in the Soke of Peterborough and was administered by Northamptonshire. The number of messuages indicates a population of between two and three thousand. If this estimate is reasonably accurate, it suggests that Stamford was the second largest town in the East Midlands; only Lincoln was larger.

Four churches are mentioned in the Survey, but only one is specifically named, St Peter's. It has not proved possible to put names to the other three. However, one of them is almost certainly All Saints in the market, and it can be conjectured that the other two were St Clement's, which stood just to the north off Scotgate, and Holy Trinity, which was on the eastern outskirts of the town. If these are the churches referred to, it suggests a degree of urban expansion even at this early date. However, it is also possible that one of the churches might have been St Michael's, as this stood within the area of the original settlement. The Survey also mentions at least one mill which, in all probability, was Kings Mill on Bath Row.

Another important fact that emerges from the Domesday Survey is that some of the most notable people in the land held property in the town. These included Edward the Confessor's queen, Edith, who held Hambleton in Rutland and an estate in Stamford consisting of several houses and St Peter's Church. Countess Judith, William the Conqueror's niece, also held a number of houses in Stamford.

The ownership of Stamford in subsequent years reflects the town's continuing links with royalty and national affairs. In 1156 Richard II granted control of Stamford, together with the castle and manor, to his friend and loyal supporter Richard du Hommet, constable of Normandy and sheriff of Rutland.

National politics in the two hundred years following the Conquest tended to revolve around controversy and conflict within the Norman ruling elite. Generally these had little impact on Stamford, though occasionally they had a direct affect on the town. After the death of Henry I in 1135 his nephew, Stephen of Blois, seized the English throne. Henry's appointed heirs, his daughter Matilda and her husband Geoffrey of Anjou, retaliated by beginning a campaign to recover their inheritance. As a result their son Henry of Anjou gained control of Normandy and invaded England in 1153. He marched with his army through the Midlands, besieging and capturing Stamford Castle whilst Stephen was investing

Ipswich castle and was unable to come to the aid of the defenders.

Stamford was frequently the meeting place for rebellious nobles and their troops. One reason for this was that Stamford was a legitimate venue for tournaments. The king licensed tournaments over a wide area stretching from Oxford bridge to Stamford bridge. Thus, under the cover of attending a tournament, the nobles were able to meet and plot. During the reign of King John and his son, Henry III, Stamford often saw the muster of rebellious lords and their troops.

During King John's reign, the Norman lords were dispossessed and, in 1205, the king gave the town to his cousin William de Warenne, in compensation for the loss of his lands in France. When William Warenne died in 1240, Henry III first kept the town in his own hands, then gave it to his son, Prince Edward, on his marriage to Eleanor of Castile. In 1275 Edward (by now Edward I) gave the town to John, son of William de Warenne and son-in-law of Henry III, and the Warenne family held it until 1347 when the last of the family died.

The town then passed to Edward III's cousin William Bohun, Earl of Northampton. After his death in 1360 it was reunited with the rest of the Warenne lands which Edward III settled on his second son Edmund Langley, Earl of Cambridge and later Duke of York. The town remained in the family of the Dukes of York until a later duke became Edward IV. He then granted it to his mother Cicely, Dowager Duchess of York. On her death it was settled on Elizabeth of York, the new queen of Henry VII. Therefore, for most of the medieval period, Stamford and Grantham (the two were linked in most of these transfers) were held in the immediate circle of the monarch's family.

It is unlikely that those who owned Stamford actually ever lived permanently in the town, although they may have visited it on occasion. Rather, they relied on bailiffs and

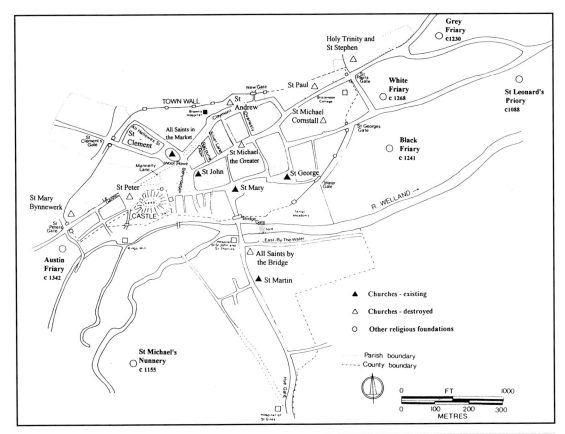

7 Map showing the extent of the medieval town, and the location of the main ecclesiastical sites.

8 This bastion which stands at the junction of Petergate and West Street is all that remains of the town walls. However the line of the walls can be traced for almost the entire circuit in the present road pattern.

stewards to manage their courts and to collect tolls, taxes and fines. The fact that Stamford was held by absentee lords provided the townspeople with the opportunity to secure a greater measure of control over their own affairs than might otherwise have been the case. Although there were often occasions when the town's view of its privileges and those of the stewards or bailiffs were not always in harmony.

It is possible that, well before 1200, the people of Stamford controlled their own local taxes and received certain tolls in support of some of the town's hospitals; the people of Stamford certainly alleged this to be the case. This may have some basis in fact since, as we have seen from the Domesday Survey of 1086, the town was divided into six wards. It is thought that each of these wards had two lawmen, with the 12 forming some kind of common council. If this was the case, then it is certainly possible that they were in a position to negotiate a measure of control over local taxes and tolls. Whatever their origin, in 1202 King John confirmed the 'ancient customs' of the borough.

The basis of Stamford's medieval prosperity was cloth. The wool produced in Leicestershire and Lincolnshire was particularly fine and in great demand. Much of that produced locally was distributed through Stamford, most of it as wool although a proportion was made up into cloth in the town. This cloth was reputed to have been of particularly good quality and is known to have been purchased for use in royal households.

It was this same wool which made Flanders the leading cloth producing region in 13th-century Europe. The difference, however, between England and Flanders was that on the continent the industry was concentrated in the great towns whereas here it was scattered throughout many small towns and villages in the east midlands, of which Stamford was but one.

The town appears to have acted more as a distribution than a manufacturing centre. It was wool merchants and exporters who dominated the town rather than weavers and dyers; although we know that weaving was carried on in the town, the extent of it is uncertain. Evidence from the Hundred Rolls shows that Stamford acted as a collecting place for the local area, and then sent wool abroad, mainly through Boston. Worsteds were produced in the town in the early 14th century.

Stamford also had a thriving pottery industry, which was based on local clay. This industry, as we have seen, probably started in the ninth century and continued well into the 13th century. The pottery, which was traded all over the country, has been found as far afield as York, London, Oxford and Bristol.

The other medieval industry, for such it was, is that of building. The limestone ridge on which Stamford is built provided excellent freestone. Although it is also worth remembering that, whilst much stone was quarried within the town, its buildings are a mixture of Stamford, Barnack and Ketton stone. Stonework was not only confined to church building.

9 Examples of Stamford ware. This pottery which was produced from the ninth to the 13th centuries was one of the first glazed wares in Northern Europe after the Roman period.

10 The Norman arch at St Mary's Hill. The adjacent sign proclaims this to be a postern gate; this is not the case as the town walls did not run in this direction. This is more likely to have been the doorway into the undercroft of the house which stood on this site or, possibly, the door into the screens passage. The arch can be dated to about 1150.

11 A number of medieval undercrofts remain in the town. This example from the early 13th century is at no. 13 St Mary's Hill.

During this period Stamford appears to have had a significant number of stone-built houses. Little early medieval domestic architecture now remains other than in fragments; such as the mis-named pack-horse arch in St Mary's Hill which in all probability is the doorway into the undercroft or the screens passage of the medieval house that once stood on the site. A number of medieval undercrofts reflects the town's commercial activity as well as testifying to the wealth of the town and a flourishing building industry.

It was for its markets that Stamford was most widely known. This role took on a wider significance in Stamford due to its heavy involvement in the international wool market. In this regard Stamford hosted important wool and cloth fairs. The cloth fair was clearly a major event and was held from mid-Lent to Easter. The fair was a trading event of some importance not only to Stamford but to the nation as a whole. It was certainly international in the sense that many foreign merchants attended it and, in 1227, the King ordered the fair bailiffs to arrest all unlicensed French merchants who attended the fair. There is evidence that the king sent his servants to the fair to buy cloth both for himself and his house-

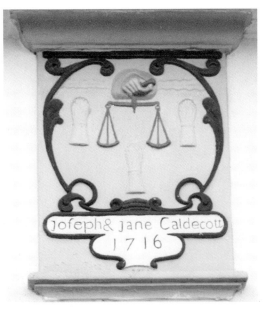

12   Date panel, St Paul's Street, showing the arms of the Bakers' Company.

hold. This was also the time for the monasteries to replenish their stocks of cloth and for nobles to buy luxury foreign goods and the newest fashions. Records show that merchants from Germany, Italy, France and the Low Countries attended the fair on a regular basis. Some, such as Eustace Malherbe and Terricus of Cologne, went so far as to buy property and settle in the town.

Equally important was the town's role as a market centre for the rural hinterland and regular markets were held for local agricultural produce, together with larger markets for livestock, corn etc. Spread throughout the town were markets which dealt in specific commodities; the 'white meat' market was held in what is now Red Lion Square; the flesh market or shambles in front of St Michael's Church; the beast market in Broad Street and the sheep market in Red Lion Square. Around

13   The north side of Lord Burghley's Hospital showing the 12th-century buttress and arch which were incorporated into the later building.

14   King's Mill. The present building was constructed *c*.1640. The original mill on this site is probably that referred to in Domesday Book.

15   Drawing of the town bridge and the guildhall from Peck's *Antiquarian Annals of Stanford*.

the market cross were the sellers of butter and eggs; the corn market stood inside St George's Gate in Cornstall. Those who did not rent a stall in one of these market places sold from baskets or from their shop windows.

As might be expected, so much commercial activity attracted a significant Jewish population to the town. They were not particularly popular, but whether this was due more to their trade as money lenders or to their often misunderstood religious practices is not clear. Certainly the Crusades championed by Richard I went some way to fostering anti-Jewish feelings as well as the more natural resentment of their wealth and privilege. In Stamford there were frequent violent incidents, particularly in the years 1189 and 1223. On a number of occasions the Jews had to take refuge in the castle and in 1242 their synagogue was burned down. Despite all this they remained in Stamford until, in common with all the Jews of the kingdom, they were forced out of the country in 1290.

There can be little doubt that the bridging of the river Trent at Newark in the second half of the 12th century had a significant impact on Stamford's trading fortunes. The erection of this bridge had the effect of altering the course of the main London to York road, so that it passed through Stamford and Grantham rather than Nottingham. This would have greatly increased the number of people passing through the town on their journeys to and from York. As the Great North Road became the established route to York and the north, the town would have seen all manner of people passing through—royalty, barons, lords, ecclesiastical dignitaries, merchants, traders and the ever-present military in the shape of knights and soldiers.

This increased traffic would have put considerable strain on the existing bridge across the Welland. The first bridge over the Welland at Stamford was built sometime in the 10th century. This became inadequate for the increased traffic, and a five-arched stone bridge with passing bays was built. In style it was probably very similar to that which now spans the river Nene at Wansford. This bridge lasted until the construction in 1845 of that presently in use.

Stamford was often chosen as the meeting place for royal councils and parliaments. On these occasions royalty would stay either at one of the friaries or at St Leonards Priory, while nobles hired residences where they could. Less eminent travellers were well provided for by the numerous inns in the town. Edward I paid many visits to the town. His wife's funeral cortège stopped here in December 1290, an event marked by the erection of an Eleanor Cross near the present Casterton Road.

Two hundred years after the Conquest Stamford had reached the zenith of its fortunes. It was one of the largest and richest towns in the country, with a population approaching five thousand. Its economy, based on wool and grain, was thriving and, as the Hundred Rolls show, its activities involved some of the biggest merchant families, including the Flemings and the Lombards. The town was also involved in the production of cloth, leather and metal products, as well as being the market centre for the surrounding region; its limestone quarries provided the raw material for a thriving building industry. That the town was undoubtedly prosperous is reflected in the level of ecclesiastical and domestic building and rebuilding.

Three

Priests and Scholars

Stamford's medieval importance was unquestionably based on trade, but also of importance was its emerging role as an ecclesiastical centre of some significance. The 14 parish churches and numerous hospitals that the town supported testify to Stamford's medieval prosperity. Equally, the monastic houses and friaries tell of the changing pattern of religion in Norman England.

As we have seen, the Domesday Survey recorded four churches in Stamford, one of which was St Peter's. The Northamptonshire Domesday Book makes reference to a place called 'Portland' where the churches of St Peter and All Saints held land. It has been suggested that this name refers to part of Stamford: if this is the case, then All Saints was clearly in existence by 1086. The other two are equally difficult to pin down. Over the years theories have been put forward which suggest that the other pre-Conquest churches were likely to have been Holy Trinity and St Clement's. However, some later historians have taken the view that, based on their proximity to the early settlement, St Michael the Greater or St George's could have been pre-Conquest foundations.

By the first half of the 11th century parish churches were being founded in increasing numbers. Their foundation was usually by landowners (or merchants) who paid for the erection of the building, endowed it with land (glebe) and provided a house for the priest. Stamford's position as a royal borough, and the absence of any overlord other than the king, meant that,

for those individuals or groups wealthy enough, there was no impediment to establishing their own church. Eventually, however, most of Stamford's churches came under the control of the monasteries, and were used as a means of extracting revenue.

Within the area encompassed by the medieval walls there were 11 parish churches, with a further two in Stamford Baron and one in the eastern suburb. Some of these churches were probably quite small and, in fact, disappeared quite early. St Michael in Cornstall is a good example, in that it was united with St George's as early as 1308. St Mary Bynnewerk had disappeared by the early years of the 15th century and St Paul's ceased to be a parish church soon after 1515. The five churches that survived into the 21st century are substantial buildings and testify to both the importance and wealth of Stamford in the Middle Ages.

St Michael the Great did, of course, last into the 20th century. Having been entirely rebuilt in 1832 following the collapse of the earlier building during alterations; it was finally declared redundant in 1965.

In addition to the parish churches there was a small number of chapels which also catered for the spiritual needs of Stamfordians. These included Burghley chapel, which lay somewhere within the present Burghley park, Bradcroft chapel and the Warenne chapel outside the Eastgate. There may also have been a chapel associated with the castle.

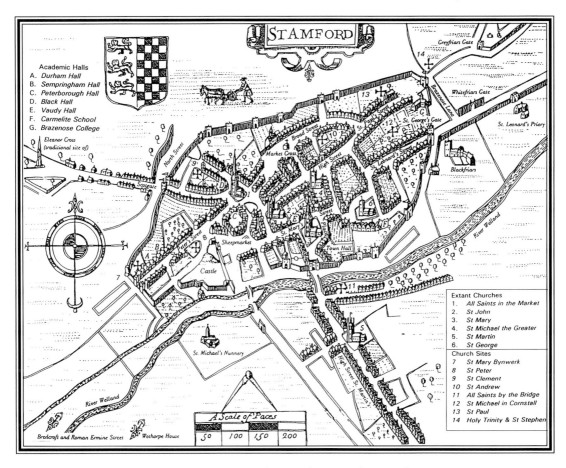

16   Map of medieval Stamford based on Speed's map of 1610.

There were three monastic houses in the town. The most important was St Leonard's Priory, a Benedictine house which is generally thought to have been founded about 1088. Fifteenth-century documents suggest that the priory was built on the site of an earlier monastery which had been founded by St Wilfred in 658 and destroyed by the Danish invasion. However, there is no evidence to support this view. Even the date of 1088 is open to debate as the first verifiable reference to St Leonard's does not occur until 1146. Then the Priory was confirmed to Durham by Pope Eugenius III. St Leonard's Priory was a cell of Durham Cathedral and was established here to manage the property belonging to the mother house, in Stamford and elsewhere in the East Midlands. As a cell of Durham, St Leonard's would also have been a place of learning for novices and may well have prepared students for further education at Durham Hall, Oxford. The priory also held the churches of St Mary and St Mary Bynnewerk. Following its dissolution in 1538, the priory had a chequered history, being used variously as a farm house, barn and tanner's yard. Excavations between 1967 and 1977 revealed an extensive range of buildings. Today, all that remains of the original church is part of the west front and the north arcade, the rest of the present structure being post-medieval.

17 The west front of St Leonard's Priory. All that remains of the early 12th–century Benedictine priory is the nave and north arcade

18 The north arcade of St Leonard's Priory.

19 *Above*. A conjectural view of St Leonard's Priory drawn by Martin Smith. This is based on the floor plan uncovered during excavations carried out between 1967 and 1972.

20 *Left*. Much of the remains of St Michael's Nunnery were destroyed when the local section of the Syston-Peterborough Railway was built in 1846. The building of Stamford High School junior department in 1973 allowed for limited excavation of the site, which produced a wide range of pottery and stone fragments. Four arches were also uncovered, one of which is photographed here.

Quite near to St Leonard's was St Mary's Priory at Newstead. This was a small house of Austin canons known to have been quite wealthy. In 1440 the priory housed only a prior and four canons.

The nunnery of St Mary and St Michael was the largest of the monastic houses, and lay to the south of the town on the site of the present Junior High School. This nunnery was founded in about 1155 by William de Waterville, abbot of Peterborough, and is said to have housed some 40 nuns. The churches of All Saints in the Market, St Clement, St Andrew and All Saints by the bridge belonged to the nunnery and St Martin's was appropriated to them in 1156. St Michael's also had a close association with the Hospital of St Thomas and St John and the leper hospital of St Giles. St Michael's was well known for its constant scandals, and for the mismanagement of its estates. It was certainly in financial difficulties well before it was dissolved in 1536.

There was another nunnery in the neighbouring parish of Wothorpe and this is often confused with St Michael's. This small house of Benedictine nuns was founded during the 12th century and lasted until 1354, when the sole remaining nun and the endowments were transferred to St Michael's.

Why these monastic houses chose Stamford is less clear. Trade has been suggested as one possibility, given the interest Lincolnshire monasteries had in the wool trade. However, there is nothing to suggest that this type of commercial activity was conducted by the Stamford houses. It is always possible, of course, that Stamford's wealth offered the prospect of patronage that was not available elsewhere.

The hospital of St John and St Thomas stood at the south end of the town bridge. The house was founded sometime between 1173 and 1180 and consisted of a master and brethren whose task it was to care for the sick and poor travellers. The hospital was originally founded by a guild of 'palmers' (pilgrims who had been to the Holy Land) but in 1194 Peterborough

21 A drawing by William Stukeley of a carved medieval female figure, found on the site of St Michael's Nunnery in 1735.

22 All Saints' Church stands in the middle of one of Stamford's medieval markets. The exact date of the foundation of the church is unknown, although it is thought to be one of the town's pre-Conquest churches. It was certainly in existence early in the reign of Henry II. Although the church was completely rebuilt in the 15th century, it still retains much 13th-century work.

23 All Saints' Church, 13th-century blank arcading on the south side.

24 St Paul's Church, now the Grammar School chapel.

Abbey assumed control. St Giles' leper hospital was also a dependency of Peterborough. It was thought that this hospital was founded in the late 12th century possibly during King Stephen's reign, as he is reputed to have made a grant of five acres from his demesne in Stamford for a hospital of lepers. Later documents record that it was undergoing repair in 1304, 1319 and again in 1332.

Also in St Martin's was the Augustinian hospital of St Sepulchre, with its chapel dedicated to St Mary Magdalen. This is thought to have stood opposite St Martin's Church and, although nothing is heard of it after 1227, the building remained until 1818.

During the first half of the 13th century friars of the mendicant orders reached Lincolnshire, possibly in the wake of Robert

Grosseteste. As Dorothy Owen has pointed out in *Church and Society in Medieval Lincolnshire*, 'generally they settled in towns where their infectious evangelical zeal attracted many penitents and much lay enthusiasm'. Stamford attracted all four of the major orders which is, in itself, unusual as even larger towns such as Leicester and Chester usually only attracted one or two.

The friars settled outside the town walls and erected substantial buildings. The Carmelites (White Friars) and Franciscans (Grey Friars) both established themselves to the east of the town. The Franciscan friary was large and attracted substantial endowments, amongst which was a 'sumptuous chapel' founded by Joan, widow of the Black Prince. Blanche Lady Wake, daughter of the Earl of Lancaster, was buried here. The

25   Grey Friars Gate, built in the mid-14th century. The gate was incorporated into a porter's lodge for the new Stamford and Rutland Infirmary in 1848.

26 *Right.* Brazenose Gate. This stands on the supposed site of Brazenose Hall where Oxford masters and students set up their rival university in 1333. However, there appears to be no medieval evidence to confirm that this was the site.

27 *Below right.* St Michael the Great. The original church was founded in the 12th century. This engraving was by R.L. Wright for Drakard's *History, c.*1822.

Dominicans (Black Friars) settled to the south-east between St Leonard's Priory and St George's Gate. This was also a large and important house and the provincial chapter of the Black Friars was held there on several occasions; it also entertained royalty. The Friars of the Sack occupied a site just outside St Peter's Gate. Sometime after the order was suppressed in 1274, the house was taken over by the Austin Friars.

Following the Dissolution, the site of the Grey Friary passed through a number of hands before being acquired by William Cecil in 1561. By this time the main buildings had already been demolished, although there were clearly still buildings on the site as they were made use of. In August 1566 Cecil recorded in his diary that the queen 'was entertained at my house, the Grey Friary, because my daughter Ann was suddenly seized with the smallpox at Burghley'. The Cecil family also acquired the sites of the White Friars, St Michael's Nunnery and St Leonard's Priory.

Although a number of early historians refer to academic halls in the town, there is no real evidence of their existence other than Sempringham Hall, which stood on the north side of St Peter's Street. The tradition that there were six other academic halls is certainly of long standing and is mentioned by Leland in the 1540s. In the 18th century both Peck and Stukeley attempted to ascribe particular buildings to these halls.

The presence of the monastic establishments, with their schools, may have been a contributory factor to one of the most celebrated

28 St Mary's Church occupies a commanding position overlooking the Welland valley. Its 13th-century tower is surmounted by a magnificent 14th-century broach spire.

29 St Martin's was rebuilt between 1480-5, replacing an earlier building of *c.*1146. This illustration is from a Sharpe and Ackerman engraving of 1856.

events of Stamford's medieval history. In the early 14th century, dissension among students at Oxford led to a number of attempts at establishing a rival institution. On the first occasion, in 1264, they moved to Northampton which proved unsuitable. Then in 1333 and 1334 they again moved from Oxford attempting to establish a collegiate hall at Stamford. Both Oxford and Cambridge universities clearly saw this as a threat and they petitioned the king, the queen and the bishop of Lincoln to outlaw the assembly at Stamford. In their petition to the queen, the Oxford staff wrote: 'Since, lady, certain persons who have obtained all their degrees from us, have now gone to Stamford, to the destruction ... of our

university, and are everyday attracting others there by their false pretences'.

This embryonic university was forced to return to Oxford by royal decree, despite a counter petition (apparently supported by Peterborough Abbey) from the clerks living in the town of Stamford. Their view was that Stamford was a place to study, 'and become proficient in greater quiet and peace by the sufferance of the noble John earl of Warenne'.

Later evidence of this episode in Stamford's history existed in the oath taken by all Oxford undergraduates until 1854 in which they had to swear that they 'will not lecture or attend lectures at Stamford, as in a university or general school or college'.

30 The east elevation of St George's Gate as drawn by J. Carter Coley *c.*1783. Until the 1730s it was known as Cornstall gate. It remained until 1805 and was the last of the town gates to be demolished.

There was a house in Stamford known as Brazenose, the gate of which was said to have been decorated with the original knocker from Brazenose Hall in Oxford. In order to recover this item of door furniture, the college bought the house in the late 19th century and took the knocker back in triumph to Oxford.

At the beginning of the 21st century Stamford's town centre churches remain substantially as they were following the reorganisation of 1548. St Martin's had been moved to the newly created diocese of Peterborough in 1541, leaving the anomaly of a town with five churches in one diocese and the sixth in another. However, this was finally resolved in 1990 when St Martin's was moved back to the diocese of Lincoln. Only St Michael's has ceased as a church, and rather unsympathetically turned into shops. This has been replaced by Christ Church, built in the 1960s to serve the burgeoning council estate to the north of the town centre. For a town of its size (population about 19,000) Stamford has been fortunate to retain, in active use, six churches, five of them medieval, when many larger centres of population have but one church.

Four

THE LATER MIDDLE AGES

THE PICTURE OF STAMFORD at the beginning of the 14th century is much less positive than it was a hundred years earlier. In 1340 the king's commissioners, when enquiring into the state of the castle, reported that: 'The castle is old and the walls decayed; within are an old tower, a great hall, a chamber with solar, a chapel, a turret and a house for a prison, all of no value'.

There is no evidence to suggest that the castle was reduced to this state as a result of military action, so we must conclude that it was no longer of any strategic importance and because of this had fallen into disuse and disrepair.

The town itself also seems to have been suffering economic difficulties and these may have started in the late 13th century. The expulsion of the Jews by Edward I in 1290 clearly affected commercial activity, as did the trade restrictions that accompanied the Hundred Years War which began in 1337. There was also a decline in demand for the traditional cloths produced by Lincoln and Stamford. Although, for a time, export of such cloth did rise, it was not sufficient to compensate for the general decline in the wool trade. Briefly, in 1353 Stamford was designated as one of the 'Staple' towns for the sale and export of wool. This status, however, was short-lived as the wool trade was undergoing revolutionary trans-formation. These changes, which breathed life into the new wool centres of East Anglia, the Cotswolds and the West Riding of Yorkshire, were to prove a considerable setback to Stamford's economic growth. In some respects Stamford's experience paralleled that of Lincoln, since this formerly great city also suffered a period of decline due to changes in the wool industry. Clearly these were difficult times for Stamford, and there is evidence to suggest that many other town centre properties were already in a state of decay.

The great fair, which had been an important part of Stamford's calendar a hundred years earlier, appears to have diminished in importance during the 14th century. Again, this is probably a direct result of the wars against France, which would have prevented merchants from attending in any number. Not only did this period see the fall of wool exports but such wool as was exported appears to have gone directly from the producers, completely by-passing the fairs. The way in which the fair had changed can be gauged by the fact that, when the king sent purchasers in 1401, it was to buy horses and no longer to buy cloth.

If the migration of Oxford students to Stamford in 1333/34 had been allowed to continue and a new university evolved this would have doubtless gone some way to restoring the town's fortunes. As it was, royal intervention ensured that this was a short-lived affair. Ultimately it appears to have had little impact on the town.

In these early years of the 14th century, the situation was to become much worse. The Black Death which swept through Europe reached England in the summer of 1348. It attained its peak in 1349, although there were later outbreaks, notably in 1361 and 1375. There is no record of how many in Stamford died in these epidemics, although we can infer from the way in which the suburbs and their churches declined that the number was substantial. Lincolnshire, and East Anglia and London, were the areas worst hit by the plague and it has been suggested that the mortality rate there was probably as high as 30 per cent.

Not everything was in decline, however. To a large extent the four friaries in the town appear to have been unaffected by the town's situation. During this difficult period they continued to attract the patronage of wealthy and noble people including Joan of Kent, mother of Richard II, and Blanche Lady Wake, daughter of the Earl of Lancaster. The buildings of the friaries were embellished and endowed to house the tombs of these wealthy patrons. Peck describes the Greyfriary as being a 'magnificent structure ... famouse for its beautiful church and steeple, which last they say, was very like that fine spire, now belonging to All Saints' church'. As has been seen, on occasion the king resided and held court at the friaries, and national ecclesiastical councils were also held there.

Stamford's connections with royalty were to bring problems of another sort. That turbulent period of history, known as the Wars of the Roses, had largely left the town unscathed, although in the winter of 1451-2 Stamford was the centre of a rising in support of the Yorkist cause. In February 1461, following her success at the battle of Wakefield, Queen Margaret moved south to meet the Earl of Warwick at St Albans. Centres of Yorkist support were plundered along the way and Stamford, which had been owned by the York family since 1363 and had been the centre of a rising involving reinforcements from other Yorkist estates in the area, found itself at the mercy of the Lancastrian army. From the Lancastrian point of view there was certainly justification for its 'sack' of the town. It had caused some concerns in 1452, when along with Grantham it became the centre of a serious rising against the government. In 1470 the town gave its support to Edward IV when the Lincolnshire Lords Wells and Willoughby rose against his rule. The two armies met just outside Stamford and fought an engagement in which the rebels were totally overwhelmed and fled the field shedding their coats as they ran. Ever after the battle was known as Loosecoat Field.

It is often suggested that many of Stamford's churches were destroyed when the town was sacked by the Lancastrians. This appears to stem from the writings of Richard Butcher and Frances Peck, both of whom wrote that the Lancastrians burned the town and destroyed many of the buildings. However, the damage said to have been caused by this event has probably been over-estimated. If the damage been as extensive as has previously been considered, there would be evidence of building activity from this period; but this is not the case.

There are other reasons why we might suggest that the sack of Stamford was not quite so damaging as suggested. There is glass in St George's and St John's churches which predates 1461 and even Yorkist symbols in the glass at St Mary's, none of which was damaged. St Martin's is the only church to have been rebuilt after the sack, but this was not until the 1480s. A gap of twenty years between the sack and the rebuilding of what was, by then, the only church south of the river argues against a significant level of damage.

31 St George's Church. The parish boundaries suggest that this may have been one of Stamford's pre-Conquest churches, but there is no evidence to support this idea. The earliest reference to the church is 1199.

Stamford's reward for its involvement in the struggles was the award of a charter of incorporation in 1462. The borough council was established under an alderman with an upper and lower council each of 12 members, who were elected by the freemen of the town. Justices of the Peace were also appointed and the town was to be represented in Parliament by two MPs. For its shield, the borough adopted the royal arms combined with those of the Warenne family. In 1481, Edward IV awarded the town a second charter. This was specifically concerned with economic issues and provided for a weekly market and two new fairs, at Corpus Christi and the feast of SS Simon and Jude. The Corporation was also given property so that it could maintain the town walls.

It would be easy to suggest that towards the end of the 15th century Stamford had declined significantly from its former economic importance. However, it is difficult to calculate the degree of such decline, as the amount of rebuilding that took place in the second half of the century suggests that the town was still faring better than many others. The eclipse in Stamford wool and the relocation of the cloth industry created something of a recession. Such trade as remained was in the hands of a few individuals whose businesses were sufficiently big to weather the storm. These included Geoffery Casterton, John Browne, William de Styanderbey and John Spicer. The poll-tax returns for 1379 reflect the prosperity of these men who were paying tax at a much higher rate than other tradesmen in the town. William Cunningham, writing on the *Growth of English Industry and Commerce*, suggests that 'There is hardly any token of general prosperity on which we may rely with more confidence than the fact that many people are able and willing to expend money on buildings'.

One of the most eminent families in the town at this time were the Brownes. As well as being wool merchants and members of the Staple of Calais, they were prominent in local

affairs. Their memorial brasses can still be seen in All Saints' Church. William Browne, the most outstanding member of the family, served the office of alderman twice, in 1466 and 1470. Leland, writing in the mid–16th century, described him as a 'merchant of very wonderfulle richnesse'.

The Browne family epitomised that personal piety characteristic of the 15th century and manifested in the building and beautification of many parish churches up and down the country. In the 1470s and 1480s John and William rebuilt much of All Saints' Church and added the magnificent spire. Also in the 1470s William Browne founded the hospital that bears his name in Broad Street. The hospital provided accommodation for 10 men and two women under the supervision of a warden and confrator. Uncharacteristically, for a man of business, Browne failed to set up the charity officially and it was left to his brother-in-law, Thomas Stokes, Canon of York, to formalise the arrangement in 1489. As Browne had no heir, on his death the business passed to his nephew Christopher. Fairly soon after this, and presumably because of Stamford's increasing provincialism, he moved the concern to London.

The Brownes, of course, were not the only substantial merchants in the town. St John's church was rebuilt by a wealthy syndicate in 1451 and St Martin's was also completely rebuilt and enlarged between 1480-5. Sir William Bruges, Garter King of Arms, made provision in his will for the rebuilding of the chancel of St George's, and for a series of stained glass windows depicting the Knights of the Garter. William Hykeham, a local baker and alderman, helped to rebuild the Corpus Christi chapel in St Mary's Church. St Michael's Church also received extensive alterations.

Not all rebuilding was ecclesiastical. There was a significant amount of domestic building undertaken at this time, although the newer buildings were more likely to be timber-framed than of stone. Typical of the new buildings

32 Browne's Hospital, built and endowed by William Browne in 1471, as a chantry with chaplains and alms for 12 poor people. During Browne's lifetime it was called Claymont Hospital. This engraving of the hospital before restoration is by R.L. Wright for Drakard's *History*, *c*.1833.

33 Browne's Hospital, *c*.1910.

34   The first mention of St John's Church is in the early years of the 13th century. Its size and location suggest that it was one of the later foundations although, in time, it was to become one of the wealthiest churches in the town.

was the timber-framed style of the *Vaults Inn* and nos. 43-44 St Mary's Street. The timber-framed building at nos. 6-7 Red Lion Square is another fine example; this is thought to have been the Browne family's woolhouse. The former All Saints' vicarage at no. 16 Barn Hill is among the last of the stone buildings from this period.

The later Middle Ages also saw a growth of guilds in the town. St Mary's guild was the oldest and in all probability the wealthiest; it met in St Mary's Church as did the guild of Corpus Christi which had been founded at about the time of the Black Death. By the early part of the 15th century the Corpus Christi guild had accumulated property throughout the town and had a guildhall on the site of no. 4 St Mary's

Place. The other parish churches also had their guilds; Holy Trinity formed a guild to support their priest who was 'very poor', St Katherine's guild met in a room over the porch of St Paul's Church. The gild at St Martin's is mentioned as early as 1389 and appears to have been responsible for the parish bull. It has been asserted that this guild later became involved with bull running but there is no real evidence for this. Certainly the Churchwarden's Accounts show that the guild still existed as a social gathering in the 18th century, and there are frequent references to the parish bull but interestingly none of these references coincide with the date of the annual bull running.

By the end of the 14th century Stamford's commercial base had undergone significant change and was concentrated far less on wool and cloth. From the records of those admitted as freemen, we can obtain some idea of the range of trades which were carried on in the town. Not everyone admitted as a freeman stated his trade, so any conclusions are tentative. Nevertheless, there are still sufficient numbers from which to make some general observations. Whilst textile workers still formed the largest group of workers, the leather workers also constituted a significant body. Other trades and occupations tended to reflect the town's role as a local market centre and a stopping place on the Great North Road. There were, for example, smiths, wrights, ironmongers, pewterers, locksmiths and goldsmiths. What might generally be referred to as service trades were represented by barbers, surgeons, servants, minstrels, cooks, notaries and scriveners.

The town was clearly at a crossroads. Those commercial activities which had contributed to its former greatness had all but disappeared. Should the town persevere with textiles and hope for better times? Or was leather working the answer? Unfortunately, neither of these options was fully exploited. At the beginning of the 16th century, therefore, the Corporation faced the problem of restoring the town's fortunes.

Five

LORDSHIP AND COMMUNITY

HISTORIANS HAVE MADE MUCH of Stamford's decline in the 15th and 16th centuries. The evidence for this, however, is by no means clear. We can identify conditions which indicate economic difficulty, but other indicators suggest that the town was managing to hold its own during difficult times. It is also possible that such decline as there was actually began much later. From the available evidence it is possible that Stamford entered the Tudor period with a reasonable measure of prosperity. Thereafter a rapid decline was experienced due partly to civil war; partly to the silting of the river and in no small measure to the effects of the Reformation. In 1541 both Stamford and Grantham were described as 'decay'd' towns.

During the 15th century Stamford's population remained static during a period of national growth. In the lay subsidy of 1524 it was ranked at 32nd with assessed wealth of about £180. While this placed it below Leicester and Lincoln it appears to have been equal, at least in wealth, with Northampton. In this subsidy, Stamford is shown as having 199 taxpayers, with a further 43 in St Martin's. If we calculate this as 243 households then Stamford was certainly not a large town.

In 1561 the privy council required from his diocesan bishop a return of the parishes and hamlets in his diocese. From this information we can obtain a fairly accurate estimate of the size of Stamford in the mid-16th century. The return for the deanery of Stamford lists the following households in each parish: St Mary 41, St Michael 52, St John 31, St George 30 and All Saints 56. This gives a total for the northern half of the town of 213 households. As St Martin's was in a different diocese it is not mentioned; but if we assume St Martin's to have remained roughly the same size, then Stamford would have been equal in size to Grantham which, at the same date, had 252 households.

Leland visited the town in 1541 and speaks of the Lancastrian sack that the town 'is not synce fully re-edified'. However, it is possible that the derelict houses he saw were the result of a shrinking population and not the ravages of war.

The town's situation appears to have prompted a number of charitable endowments. In the 1570s the Corporation established a poor house. In 1597 William Cecil re-founded the hospital of St John and St Thomas as an almshouse. This later became known as Lord Burghley's Hospital. Twelve years later, in 1609, Thomas Cecil granted manorial rights in East and West Deeping to the Corporation to assist in apprenticing the youth of Stamford into various occupations.

Whilst changes within the wool industry were clearly an important factor in Stamford's economic decline, the town should have been able to weather that particular storm if other industries had emerged to supplant it. No industry of any significance came along to take over from the woollen industry and the town council turned its back on the one possible contender, that of leather. Had consideration been given to the tanning of leather on a large scale (it was already carried on in a small way), the town may have regained its prosperity and it may have become another Kettering or Northampton. Some small industries flourished, including bell founding, but none of any significance.

In the 1560s William Cecil supported an attempt to start a canvas-weaving industry in the town, together with a proposal for the building of a hemp-beating mill which, it was suggested, would beat enough hemp to employ 300-400 people. Clearly this was too big a scheme, since the town had nothing like enough workers to man it. Another, more modest, suggestion was the purchase of 20-40 stones of hemp to set the poor to work. The use of hemp as a raw material probably suggested itself because Stamford sat between the two hemp-growing areas—the Fens in the east and Rockingham forest in the west. There is no real indication of how successful this scheme was, but by the end of the 17th century there were only nine hemp dressers and one roper recorded in the town.

A more fruitful proposition was to settle Dutch immigrants in the town. A number of towns in the east and south-east were at this time inviting refugees, persecuted for their religion, to come over from France and Flanders. It is interesting that these invitations were almost always from towns which had fallen on hard times. In trying to attract artisans who would bring new skills they might also bring new wealth to the town. The craftsmen invited to Stamford were weavers of bays, stammets, fustians, carpets etc., hatters, the makers of rope, coffers, knives, locks and metal workers. The Dutch accepted the offer but requested permission to bring 20 households rather than the 10 that Cecil had provided accommodation for. The scheme made some headway and, in 1572, correspondence was in progress between Cecil and Caspar Vosbergh concerning the endowment of a church in the town, but,

despite financial incentives from Cecil, it does not appear to have been particularly successful.

Stamford was unfortunately unable to capitalise on one of the few developments which might have improved its fortunes much earlier than it did. As the fens were drained, sheep-grazing moved further to the east and the lime-stone heathlands were put to the plough. Barley for malting became the principal crop. The silted state of the Welland, however, meant that it was not possible to develop the malting trade within the town. In 1570 the council secured an Act of Parliament to make the river navigable, but practical difficulties and lack of money meant that it would be ninety years and another Act of Parliament before this was fully effected.

As we have seen, Stamford's population remained static at a time of national growth. The general increase experienced elsewhere created a shortage of land and food, which inevitably forced up prices. In the first forty years of the century food prices rose eightfold whilst wages rose only threefold. Standards of living must have dropped significantly during these years. Many people were forced onto the road to seek work and Stamford's position on the Great North Road ensured that it saw more than its fair share of vagrants seeking work. In 1547 the town council were clearly concerned by the unemployment and poverty in the town and issued an ordinance that no one should give work to strangers while natives of Stamford were without work. In 1584, when money had to be raised to pay the fifteenth (a tax on moveable property), the town could not pay and decided to lease out the tenter meadows to help raise the money. In 1624, Lord Keeper Lincoln in a letter to Secretary Conway refers to the '... poor decayed town of Stamford' and recommends their petition for exemption from paying the fifteenth.

During the 16th century Stamford's role as a market centre for the local area appears to have diminished as competition from other towns grew. For many local farmers, Stamford was just one of the markets they visited. In many cases, much of the local produce went straight to the London markets. Stamford Fair, however, was clearly still both well known and of some importance. Shakespeare refers to it in Henry IV when Justice Shallow enquired of 'a good yoke of bullocks at Stamford Fair?'.

The other major factors in Stamford's economic fortunes were the Dissolution and Reformation and their effect on the town's religious institutions. Although doubtless influenced by reformists, humanism and emerging continental Protestantism, the Reformation in England was dominated by Henry VIII. He was determined to have at his disposal the economic power of the church. The desire for an annulment of his marriage to Catherine of Aragon, and his inability to obtain it from the Pope, was another decisive factor.

This resulted in a number of acts that severed the link with Rome and made him supreme head of the church in England. The monasteries and friaries, with their wealth, land, papal exemptions and loyalties, were clearly a threat to the stability of this new regime and needed to be removed. Their dissolution proved advantageous to the king in a number of ways, not least because the sale of monastic lands would provide much needed income for the royal coffers.

Lincolnshire had a large number of religious houses and their closure did not pass without protest. In October 1536 opposition broke out in the north of the county, with a call to return to the Catholic faith. This protest was as much about seeking redress for fiscal, political and economic grievances as it was about the defence of the monasteries. The rising, known as the Pilgrimage of Grace, was quickly subdued and on 13 October the rebels surrendered when they heard that the Duke of Suffolk was at Stamford with an armed force; just as Yorkshire and the northern counties were about to rise. By this time St Leonard's and Newstead priories together with St Michael's Nunnery had been dissolved as had the four friaries. Within the

town itself 'reformed' opinion was openly and sometimes violently expressed. On one occasion a Dominican friar preached in St Martin's for the retention of orthodoxy and was attacked by the congregation for his trouble. In 1550 (during Edward VI's reign) Hugh Latimer could visit the town and preach in the cause of the Reformation with official sanction.

One Stamford institution to survive the Reformation was the grammar school. This had been founded under the will of William Radcliffe in 1532 as a chantry school. That is, a priest-schoolmaster combined instruction with praying for the dead and in particular for William Radcliffe. That the school was not swept away with other chantries is said to be due to the intervention of William Cecil. In September 1548, when Cecil was Somerset's secretary, two private Acts of Parliament were passed, one of which confirmed the grouping of the Stamford parishes and the other confirmed the continuance of the grammar school. It seems likely that Cecil was directly involved in ensuring that his old school, which by this time was well established in the old St Paul's Church, survived.

Mention has already been made of the part played in town affairs by William Cecil. It was during the early part of the 16th century that members of the Cecil family first settled in the Stamford area. Just as Lincoln owed much to the patronage of Cardinal Wolsey, so Stamford's fortunes were to become closely linked to those of the Cecil family.

The forebears of William Cecil, Lord Burghley, came from a small manor on the Welsh border with Herefordshire. A younger son, David, like all younger sons had to make his own way in the world. He was the first member of the family to come to Stamford, although exactly why is not clear. We do know that he was steward to Lady Margaret Beaufort and that he married Alice Dickons, the daughter of John Dickons, a well-to-do Stamford merchant. In 1506, he acquired an estate in the county and over the next ten

35 William Cecil, Lord Burghley (1520-98), Lord High Treasurer of England. Portrait by Marcus Gheeraerts of Lord Burghley in the robes of a Knight of the Garter, holding his wand of office.

36 Burghley House was built by William Cecil, Lord Burghley. Built on the site of a 12th-century monastery, the house took over thirty-five years to complete.

years or so was favoured with a number of crown offices as a result of having joined with Henry Tudor in his campaigns for the Crown. In 1531 he became sheriff of Northamptonshire. He was alderman of Stamford in 1506-15 and again in 1526.

David's elder son Richard was a country gentleman and became sheriff of Rutland. In 1527 he bought the manor of Little Burghley. Richard's wife was Jane Heckington of Bourne. It was at Bourne, in 1520, that she gave birth to William Cecil.

Cecil was educated at Grantham, Stamford grammar school, St John's College Cambridge and, later, at Gray's Inn. He was elected to parliament in 1547. He found his way to court through the patronage of, firstly, the Duke of Somerset, to whom he was appointed secretary in 1548. Through the interest of the Duke of Northumberland, he became Principle Secretary of State on the accession of Elizabeth I.

In the 1550s, Cecil began the building of two mansions; one for himself at Theobalds, near Cheshunt in Hertfordshire, and the other

37 The monument to William Cecil in St Martin's Church. A splendid Renaissance example in marble and alabaster, it has been described as 'one of the finest examples of its kind in existence'. The monument is attributed to Cornelius Cure, and is close in style to his monument to Mary, Queen of Scots in Westminster Abbey.

38-40 Although Stamford is a 'stone-built' town, there are still numerous examples of timber-framed buildings. *Above left.* This 16th-century timber-framed house in St Mary's Street was for many years the *Cross Keys Inn*. *Above right.* A timber-framed house in St Peter's Street, built *c.*1660. *Below left.* Many people daily walk past this timber jetty without realising it. It once stood in a passage to the side of Gothic House, but has now been incorporated into Walker's Book Shop.

41 After the Dissolution, the manor of Wothorpe was acquired by Richard Cecil. In the early 17th century Thomas Cecil built Wothorpe House as a dower house.

42 The *Millstone Inn*, All Saints' Street, typical of the many inns catering for the market trade. A carriage entrance at the west end of the building has been blocked to provide additional accommodation.

for his mother at Little Burghley. Work on Burghley House was probably started in 1555 when it is known that the east range was under construction; but it was to be another 32 years before the house was finished.

Cecil did not spend a great deal of time at Burghley, although this did not inhibit his involvement in local affairs or his exercising his authority over Stamford. He continued to add to the family's holdings and acquired a number of estates in the area. In 1560 he acquired Stamford Baron which had been held by Peterborough Abbey until the Reformation and, in the following year, much to the chagrin of the town council, he acquired from the Crown the lordship of the manor of Stamford together with the fee farm and the tolls. This particular acquisition caused great ill feeling, as the council had originally asked Cecil to acquire it for the town. Cecil became Recorder

of the town and, like his predecessors, nominated the town's two MPs. In the years between 1504 and 1589 five members of Cecil's family represented Stamford in Parliament while other MPs were chosen from friends and relatives. The appointment of the aldermen and other town officials was also controlled by Cecil, as was the nomination of master at the Grammar School. The final stamp of Cecil authority came in 1593 when all these privileges were confirmed in Stamford's constitution, and by-laws were introduced to facilitate his control of borough affairs.

The Cecil influence on Stamford over the next 400 years was substantial and manifested itself in a number of ways. The powers of land ownership, patronage, coercion, paternalism and corruption were all to play their part in the long-term relationship between Stamford and the Lords of Burghley.

43   Hudd's Mill was built during the first half of the 17th century and remained in use until 1900.

44   Lord Burghley's Hospital occupies the site of the former hospital of St Thomas and St John which was founded *c.*1170–80. After the Dissolution it was purchased by William Cecil, and part of it was maintained as an almshouse until 1597 when Cecil formally endowed it. The new almshouse accommodated 13 men, one of whom served as the warden. The building at the east end is late 16th- or early 17th-century and incorporates part of the structure of the early hospital. A new west range was added *c.*1616. In the ensuing years several alterations were made, the last being in 1964.

William Cecil died in 1598 and his splendid Renaissance monument, described as 'one of the finest examples of its kind in existence', dominates the chancel of St Martin's Church. Of his two sons, Robert Cecil assumed the mantle of his father's professional responsibilities and gave up the family house at Theobalds in favour of Hatfield House; the elder son, Thomas, inherited Burghley. As he chose to live at Burghley, which had been the home of his mother, it was necessary for him to build another house for widows of the family. For this purpose he built Wothorpe House, about a mile to the south-west of Stamford. In 1605, as a reward for their loyalty to the Crown, James I created

Thomas 1st Earl of Exeter and his brother Robert became Earl of Salisbury.

At the height of its fortunes the town supported 14 parish churches. These were reduced to 10 in 1515. The majority must have been small and not well endowed. From the available population estimates, it also seems clear that they cannot have had very large congregations. In all probability, the smaller churches only catered for the spiritual needs of their merchant benefactor, his family and his employees.

If we accept a decline in the town's population during the early 15th century, then this would obviously have affected the size of church congregations and have had a debilitating effect on income. The 16th century therefore saw a gradual amalgamation of parishes, culminating in a final rationalisation in 1548 when the number of churches was reduced to six. That these parishes were amalgamated in relation to a declining population is supported by a petition of 1548 which cites this as a principal reason. The fact that it was the peripheral churches which closed first, followed by a general contraction towards the centre of the town, helps to support this view.

Many earlier historians, particularly those in the 19th century, saw the closure of many of the town's churches as a clear indication of its decline, but this can be viewed in two ways. Certainly the loss of eight churches tells of a considerable change in circumstances. Yet, if we consider the town's parish churches as an indicator of its relative prosperity, it is possible to suggest a gradual contraction of the town rather than a sudden slide into urban decay.

Stamford could still boast six parish churches, whereas many larger towns had but one. The reduction in church provision also sat more easily with the ethos of the post-Henrician English church order.

Stamford was still an important stopping place on the Great North Road and was the eighth stage on the postal route to the north. However, at this time, traffic was not frequent enough to make an impact on the local economy, although a number of inns catered for such travellers as there were. These included the *George*, the *Old Swan*, the *Black Bull*, the *Angel of the Hoop* and the *Blue Bell*; the latter was a large inn that occupied much of the east side of Ironmonger Street. Royalty continued to be occasional visitors and Henry VIII passed through on three occasions (1528, 1532 and 1539); Queen Elizabeth was entertained by Lord Burghley at Whitefriars in 1566; James I passed through on his way to Scotland in 1602 and Charles I visited the town in 1633 and 1634.

Six

CIVIL WAR

THE TOWN AT THE BEGINNING of the 17th century, like so many other English towns, was clearly weakened by economic recession which, in turn, led to poverty, malnutrition and poor living conditions. Such conditions were fertile breeding grounds for disease. The town had been visited by the plague in 1574, 1581-2 and, according to Burton, 1602. However, none of these would compare with the epidemic of 1604 which, it is said, wiped out one third of the town's population.

The corporation tried to control the out-break but, as is often the case, they did too little too late. Visitors to the town were banned and those who caught the disease were ordered to stay indoors. The council ordered that a 'Cabbin should be erected and built wherein persons infected with the sickness called the Plague shoulde be kepte and mayneteyned'. The healthy were also told not to visit nearby infected towns; nor were residents to 'leave the town because some houses were affected with plague, on payment of fines'. Despite these precautions, in that year some 600 people were buried compared with the more usual thirty to forty.

From Edward Wells, a shoemaker of St Peter's parish, we can gain some insight into the devastating effects of the plague. In the burial register of All Saints we find that Goodwife Wells wife was buried on 21 August 1604 and Edward Wells himself was buried on 24 August; his daughter Dorothy was buried on the 26th and his son Edward on the 30th.

In this one family we can see the tragic consequences of this virulent disease.

In his will Wells left in trust to the parish of All Saints his house and lands, so that 'the yearly rent and benefits arising thereof should be faithfully and duly employed towards the maintenance of a petty school within the said parish; for such children as shall be poor and freeborn within the said town; to the full and complete number of so many as the rent of the said house and land shall discharge their teaching ...'. This school became known as Wells Petty School and, later, All Saints School. Richard Snowden, vicar of St John's, also died of the plague and in his will gave land and property for the establishment and maintenance of an almshouse for seven poor widows. This almshouse was rebuilt in 1823 and still stands in Scotgate although, at present, it is no longer in use as an almshouse.

Although the plague was to trouble other parts of the country throughout the 17th century, Stamford took strict precautions to prevent its recurrence. These were reasonably successful and the town was spared further major outbreaks.

Lady Dorothy Cecil also died in 1604 and in her will left property in trust for providing 'two proper persons to teach poor children to read English and knit ...'. This school became known as St Martin's School and continued its existence until December 1962.

In this early part of the 17th century there was still no real prospect of economic improvement, and precious little investment in the town. The Norris family established a bell foundry in 1603, which became quite important within the East Midlands, but this was the exception rather than the rule. The problem was that there was no solid base for recovery.

Despite these many setbacks, Stamford's situation was beginning to improve. Whilst there is evidence to show that after 1604 the town's population began to grow, recovery was slow and, as we have seen, the town was still being described as 'decayed' in 1624.

Balanced against Lord Keeper Lincoln's description of the town is one made 13 years later by Camden who in 1637 recorded that Stamford was '... a town well peopled and of great resort, endowed with sundry immunities and walled about'. Acknowledging the damage done by the Lancastrians in 1461, Camden observes that the town has not since been able to recover its ancient dignity '... and yet now is in good estate'. Camden's description of Stamford in the early part of the 17th century is altogether more positive and appears to reflect a town that was coming to terms with the loss of its earlier status.

However, difficult times were at hand which would further delay any prospect of economic recovery. The quarrels between king and parliament culminated in the Civil War and the king raised his standard at Nottingham on 20 August 1642. Although the long-term causes of the Civil War can be traced back to the economic, social and religious changes of the 16th century, the more immediate causes lay in the breakdown of relationships between the king and parliament.

It is difficult to be certain about local loyalties; there was division and support for both sides. Stamford was not wholly royalist as has often been alleged, neither was puritanism endemic in the town. This is exemplified by the town's two members of parliament. Thomas Hatcher from Careby was a parliamentarian as was John Weaver who was MP for Stamford in all parliaments from 1645 to 1659. Geoffrey

Palmer, on the other hand, was a committed royalist. He served in the royalist parliament from 1643-4. Palmer would almost certainly have been supported by the Berties of Grimsthorpe and the Noels of Exton Hall, as both of these leading local families were firmly royalist. Robert Bertie, 1st Earl of Lindsey and a general in the king's army, was killed at the battle of Edgehill in 1642.

The polarity between John Weaver and Geoffrey Palmer mirrors the dilemma that must have faced ordinary Stamfordians when it came to the question of choosing sides. In different circumstances people might have taken their lead from the person who exerted most influence over them, the Earl of Exeter. However the 3rd Earl died in 1643 and John Cecil, the 4th Earl, was in his minority at the outbreak of the war. Not only did this mean that the Cecils avoided an open declaration of allegiance, but also that the alderman and burgesses also avoided having to cast their lot with one side or the other. In reality, many families in Stamford probably went about their daily lives doing their best to stay out of the conflict.

The political position of the Cecils at the time is difficult to assess. Traditionally the family were Anglican protestant and as such were likely to have disliked Charles I's Laudian reforms. In 1599, Thomas Cecil, as president of the Council of the North, was charged with the reduction of recusant gentry and the hunting down of papists and priests, a task which he undertook with some vigour. However, whether this would have been sufficient for them to have opposed the king is not known. The 3rd Earl was certainly active in parliament prior to his death, and we might conjecture that when the time came he would have declared for parliament. Certainly the Hatfield branch of the family supported the parliamentarian cause, as did the Grey family who had inherited the Manor of Stamford from the Cecils.

Stamford's position astride the Great North Road was to prove a significant factor

45 The *George Hotel* was known to have been in existence before 1541. The earliest part of the present building is the east range which dates from *c.*1600. The building was re-fronted in 1724 by George Portwood for the Earl of Exeter. During the Civil War the hotel would no doubt have provided accommodation for both Royalist and Parliamentarian troops as they moved up and down the strategically important Great North Road.

in its involvement in the civil wars of the 1640s. It did not suffer prolonged sieges in the way that its neighbours Newark and Crowland did, neither were there any significant battles fought in the immediate vicinity. However, its position on the main route to the north and its proximity to the royalist garrisons of Belvoir and Newark ensured that the troops of both armies were regularly in the town. To the royalists their garrison at Newark was particularly important as it guarded the road to the north, and the Earl of Newcastle's headquarters in Yorkshire.

The Great North Road therefore was strategically important to both sides.

Stamford's first experience of occupation by troops followed the royalist victory at Ancaster Heath on 11 April 1643. This victory allowed the royalists not only to occupy Grantham, but also to extend their influence southwards to Stamford and Peterborough. Having done this they were able to pose a distinct military threat to the Eastern Association's Fenland frontier as well as plunder and impose exactions from Stamford,

Peterborough and the surrounding parts of Northamptonshire.

Parliament clearly needed to deal quickly with this royalist threat to the eastern counties, and despatched Cromwell to eject the cavaliers from Stamford. Cromwell's rapid approach seems to have taken the royalist troops by surprise and, although there had been some attempt to fortify the town, they clearly realised that it was indefensible and took refuge firstly in Wothorpe House and then Burghley House. The advantage in this encounter lay wholly with Cromwell; Burghley, the country house *par excellence*, is not one that lends itself to defence against artillery and this must have been evident to those taking refuge inside. By the time the siege began at 2 a.m. on 24 July, Cromwell had been joined by Colonel Hebard, Colonel Palgrave and, possibly, Sir Samuel Luke, bringing the number of parliamentary troops to between three and four thousand, plus artillery pieces.

Considerably outnumbered, the royalists offered stiff resistance and, after a time, Cromwell, who needed to bring the matter to a swift conclusion, attempted to parley with them. His offer to allow them to leave Burghley, but without their arms, was rejected: they would neither take nor give quarter. But by the early afternoon the situation had changed and the royalists surrendered. Despite the rejection of Cromwell's terms, strict orders were given that none of the royalists was to be harmed.

In official reports parliament asserted that Burghley was garrisoned for the king, but this appears to be incorrect. The evidence shows that Burghley was occupied by the royalists on this one occasion only, and that they took refuge there because they were unable to defend the town. Local tradition says that, following the surrender at Burghley, Lady Frances Wingfield, a resident of St Martin's and a relation of Cromwell's, dissuaded him from his intention to burn the town. This seems improbable. Cromwell's troops were desperately needed at

Gainsborough and the fact that Cromwell rejoined Sir John Meldrum at North Scarle by the 27th suggests that he moved north as soon as his task at Stamford was accomplished.

The protracted siege at Newark in 1645 was sustained at great cost and the royalist forces took every opportunity to raid the neighbouring areas of Lincolnshire and Nottinghamshire to raise money for the cause. Stamford was left in a particularly vulnerable position. In answer to a petition from 'divers well affected people of Stamford', parliament wrote to the governor of Crowland in August 1645 drawing his attention to the fact that the royalists had recently exacted £200 from Stamford and, as the town could not pay the rest of their demand, they had abducted the alderman and 'others of the best affected people there'. As the alderman was obviously being held for ransom, parliament instructed the governor to seize a number of royalists so that they could be used to secure the release of the Stamford people.

The continual passage of parliamentary troops, together with royalist raids, placed a heavy financial burden on the people of Stamford. Forced payments to the royalists did not lessen their liability to pay the taxation levied by parliament. From early in 1644, the county as a whole was taxed at the rate of £2,800 per month and Stamford was expected to pay its share. In addition, local forms of taxation such as the church rate and poor rate still had to be paid. Although most of the town would have been suffering financial hardship, there was no sympathy from the council who were quick to issue distraint warrants against those who could not pay.

The other heavy cost placed on the town was that of 'free quartering', that is, providing food and lodging for troops passing through the town. The general shortage of funds and the consequent shortage of army pay led both sides to exploit and abuse this system. In theory, householders providing food and lodging should have been reimbursed at the rate of about 8d.

per day. In practice, they were seldom paid since the local army commanders had no money. Stamford's particular problem was not only convoys passing through, but also the fact that large numbers of troops used it as a mustering point.

Throughout the course of the war Stamford was to suffer the continual passing and re-passing of troops. The king himself was in the town on at least three occasions, twice openly and once secretly. Charles passed through the town in 1642 on his way to York and whilst there issued a proclamation against the papists. On 23 August 1645 he was there again at the head of a large body of troops. On this occasion the king was moving south from Doncaster to Huntingdon. The king's most celebrated visit, for Stamfordians at least, was in 1646. Charles, having escaped from the parliamentary army at Oxford on 27 April, was making his way north with Michael Hudson and Mr Ashburnham with the intention of surrendering to the Scots at Southwell. By 3 May, having roamed the country for a week, he reached Stamford where, having taken a circuitous route to enter the town, he found lodging with the Cave family at Blackfriars. Local tradition has it that he stayed in a house in Barn Hill; however, this is not the case. Michael Hudson testified that the 'King was at noe gentleman's house but Mr Cave's in Stamford'. The king remained in Stamford for the whole of the next day before leaving late at night to continue his journey north. Charles' expectation of Scottish support was sadly misplaced. In the event they sold him to parliament for £400,000, bringing the first Civil War to an end.

During 1643 and 1644 the Earl of Manchester's troops devoted their energies to clearing Lincolnshire of royalist forces to secure their hold on the eastern counties. With one notable exception, for the remainder of the Civil War, Stamford's experiences revolved around the continual coming and going of parliamentary forces and the not infrequent raids by royalist troops from Belvoir and Newark. The exception was in June 1648, when the country drifted into what became known as the second Civil War. Dr Michael Hudson, the king's scoutmaster-general and rector of Uffington, and Thomas Styles the rector of Crowland, together with Richard Wolph, a well known local royalist, and John Ashburnham of Sussex, were raising troops in Stamford at the time of the annual fair, intending to surprise the Crowland garrison. However, before they could carry out their plan, troops were sent from Leicester under Colonel Wayte to suppress the rising.

The threat posed by Hudson and Styles was clearly taken seriously; troops from Belvoir, Lincolnshire and Northamptonshire were rapidly deployed to Stamford in support of Colonel Wayte. The rising was a short-lived affair and was quickly put down. Although some sixty prisoners were taken, Styles managed to escape. Hudson, on the other hand, took refuge in Woodcroft House near Etton where, having been refused quarter, he was butchered to death.

The end of the first Civil War did not signal a return to normality for towns such as Stamford. Parliament, mindful of the need to restore order, embarked on a programme of radical religious and constitutional policies. In October 1647 the council were instructed to eject from office anyone who had supported the royalist cause and replace them with people loyal to parliament. This resulted in 14 of the 37 members of the council being dismissed. Some of them were reinstated at the Restoration, when those who had taken their place in 1647 were similarly dismissed. Purges such as this were not new to the town. In 1644 all the clergy north of the river had been ejected from their livings on charges of supporting the king, and 'Godlie and orthodox divines' appointed in their place.

How Stamford fared under the Commonwealth and Protectorate is not entirely clear. There was a flurry of military activity in south

Lincolnshire in 1655, and the formation of what appears to have been a voluntary militia under Colonel Alexander Blake; who, acting on a commission from Cromwell, raised a party of horse to 'secure these parts'. There was also some attempt to impose puritan standards on the town. In the interests of 'Godly reformation' the number of licences issued to victualling houses was reduced and some twenty inn holders were given notice to quit. The races were also abolished, as elsewhere in the country. Plans were drawn up to unite the parishes of St John and St Michael and, later, the parishes of St Mary and St George. Both these schemes were suggested largely on the grounds of poverty and the small size of some parishes; however, neither was carried out.

For the most part, the town appears to have carried on with little change. The markets continued as they had always done and admissions to freedom continued with little variation in the trades represented, which suggests little change in the economic life of the town. Despite the loss of some twenty inns in the purge of 1655, there were still 40 victuallers operating in the town. Given a population of under two thousand, many of these inns must have existed for the market trade. However, the town was not so well off that it could afford to be charitable. In 1657, there was an influx of people from other parts of the country begging in the town, and the council issued instructions that they were to be arrested and committed to the house of correction. Nevertheless, local trade must have been reasonably buoyant since, as early as 1650,

the council were seeking to improve the river Welland. Stamford seems to have survived the war far better than might have been expected, particularly during the early years when military activity was at its greatest. Following Charles II's defeat at Worcester in 1651 and the final collapse of the royalist cause, Stamford carried on as it had always done and quietly coped with its changed circumstances.

The Restoration heralded a new phase in Stamford's fortunes. This is reflected in the house built by Daniel Wigmore in 1674 at no. 19 St George's Square. Undoubtedly, this is the most distinguished house of its time and it heralded an exciting era in Stamford's architectural development. Writing in 1697 Celia Fiennes described Stamford 'as fine a built town all of stone as may be seen ... much finer than Cambridge'.

An increasing amount of building was being undertaken and, on numerous occasions, the council passed by-laws aimed at regulating building more closely. For example, in 1675 they ordered that tiles and slates must be used for all new buildings: presumably a fire precaution following serious fires in the town.

By the end of the 17th century Stamford had undergone significant changes to its status and economy, and was beginning to emerge as a commercial centre for the local area. From 1664, the river Welland was navigable again, which provided impetus for local trade. As long-distance coaching became more common, this too provided new opportunities for commercial growth.

Seven

GEORGIAN ELEGANCE

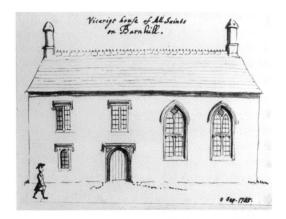

THE 18TH CENTURY bequeathed Stamford a legacy which placed it in the forefront of Georgian towns: a metamorphosis which transformed it from a decayed borough into what has been described as the 'Georgian town *par exellence*'. Interestingly, descriptions of the town in the 18th century are conflicting. To Thoresby, the Yorkshire antiquary, Stamford was a 'scurvy dear town'. William Stukeley, on the other hand, found Stamford extremely pleasant. He attended two music clubs a week where he smoked a pipe, drank a dish of coffee and was well entertained, finding it 'a true life, not the stink and noise and nonsense of London'. Defoe described Stamford as 'a very fair, well built, considerable and wealthy town'.

From our vantage point in the 21st century, we are apt to look back on the 18th century as a period of elegance. Whilst in some senses this is true, we should not forget that Georgian towns were often dirty, frequently

46 *Above right.* No. 16 Barn Hill, formerly All Saints' Vicarage, was built in the late 15th century. Originally it had an open hall at its south end possibly lit by two Gothic windows. This is suggested in this re-constructed drawing by William Stukeley.

47 *Right.* No. 19 St George's Square was built in 1674, possibly for Daniel Wigmore, a woollen draper and mercer. The building of such an imposing house, after a period of economic depression, is seen by many historians as signalling a change in the town's fortunes.

51

YORK Four Days Stage-Coach.

Begins on Friday the 12th of April 1706

ALL that are desirous to pass from London to York, or from York to London or any other Place on that Road. Let them Repair to the Black Swan in Holbourn in London and to the Black Swan in Coney-street in York

At both which Places they may be received in a Stage Coach every Monday, Wednesday and Friday, which performs the whole Journey in Four Days, (if God permits.) And sets forth at Five in the Morning. And returns from York to Stamford in two days, and from Stamford by Huntington to London in two days more. And the like Stages on their return.

Allowing each Passenger 14 a weight, and all above 3d a Pound

Performed By { Benjamin Kingman
Henry Harrison,
Walter Bayne's

Also this gives Notice that Newcastle Stage Coach, sets out from York, every Monday, and Friday, and from Newcastle every Monday, and Friday.

Rec'd in pt. 05.00. of Mr. Bodmifod for 5 for Monday the 3 of June 1706

48   An early 18th-century coaching advertisement.

smelly and the traffic was a hazard. In the early part of the 18th century the Stamford street scene consisted of old timber-frame tenements and medieval buildings which had been adapted for fresh uses; there were even farms with barns and hovels within the town area. The small size of 18th-century towns meant that the country was never far away. Fields and farms, the smell of new mown hay or of a farmyard midden, were the shared experiences of most townsmen. The common fields of Stamford, some 1,700 acres of arable, meadow and pasture, were not finally enclosed until 1875. The majority of tenants on this land were not farmers but Stamford tradesmen and craftsmen.

The consequences of improved road travel brought about by the turnpikes were many and varied. Stamford became an important centre for social assembly, particularly for the gentry of the surrounding area; it became a focal point for commerce and exchange; and the coaching inns brought many travellers who patronised local businesses. All this led to increased wealth; because much of this derived from shopkeeper prosperity, which enhanced the status of the individual, this was reflected in the town's fashionable new buildings.

The revival of Stamford, particularly after 1720, created one of the loveliest Georgian towns in England, even though the preservation of its open fields allowed no spacious crescents and few grand terraces—the main exception being Rutland Terrace (built 1829-31). The 9th Earl of Exeter was responsible for the systematic rebuilding, to a uniform design, through a series of individual buildings: seven blocks of new houses built in St Mary's Hill and St Mary's Street. Rebuilding on this scale was the exception rather than the rule. Given the constraints on space within the town, any new building could only be undertaken at the expense of the demolition of older buildings to make way for them. In many cases existing buildings were re-fronted; timber-framed buildings became quite unfashionable at this time, stone being the order of the day. Many timber-framed houses in the town were plastered over and their jetties under-built. No. 33 Broad Street is a good example of a building which has been updated in this way. Improvements to the town's amenities were also undertaken. In 1694 Daniel Denhill was commissioned to carry water by 'engines and other instruments' from the river to the market cross and erect cisterns there. It was also intended to pipe water to the houses of those who could afford to pay for it. Denhill obviously did not complete the job as a fresh agreement to do the same thing was made with William Yarnold in 1697.

Stamford's increasing wealth was very much centred on the emergent middle classes, the group which undertook most of the new building and rebuilding. In a town with so many fine buildings from the period, nos. 14-17 High Street, built as a three-storey terrace in about 1700, not only deserves special mention as a fine building but as probably the largest building project that had been undertaken in the town for some years. No. 3 All Saints Place also stands out as another fine example of early 18th-century building.

Much of Stamford's 18th-century prosperity can be attributed to its position astride the Great North Road. Although the 18th century saw a dramatic rise in coach travel, there had been regular coach services from Stamford to London since at least 1685. At that time the journey from the *George Inn* at Aldersgate to Stamford took two days at a cost of 20s. The journey from Stamford to York took a further two days. The improvements in roads produced by the turnpike trusts made it possible for horse-drawn coaches to be used more extensively and, by 1769, it was possible to travel from Stamford to London (via Royston) in a day. The fare for those travelling inside the coach was 16s. By 1776 the regular journey from London to Edinburgh was done in four days. Royal mail coaches did not start

49 The association of the Great North Road with coaching has resulted in a number of re-enactments of those long gone days. Here a coach and four is seen passing through Red Lion Square heading for the *George*.

running until about 1784 and before this the post was carried by post-boys on horseback. By 1786, the mail-coach routes had spread via the Great North Road into Lincolnshire.

In 1792 the 'Original Stamford Fly' regularly did Stamford to London in 16 hours. As road conditions improved so did the performance of the stage coaches, and by 1832 London to Edinburgh could be accomplished in 42 hours 32 minutes.

During the century responsibility for the maintenance of roads passed from the parishes to the turnpike trusts and all of Lincolnshire's main towns had turnpike connections by 1765. Although this led to a general improvement in the county's roads, the system was still dependent on the effectiveness of the trustees, and on competing interests. The work of the turnpike trusts was not always satisfactory. The *Evening Mail* of 15 April 1799 reported: 'Thursday last the York Mail coach was overturned by the wheel sinking into a hole in the road between Stamford and Witham Common. By the accident the guard, Robert Northern had his leg broken. The road is so full of holes that it is dangerous to drive above 6 mph; the mail coach should do 8 mph ...' Such reports were not uncommon at the time.

The peak year for the coaching trade in Stamford was 1830 with some 40 mail and 30 stage coaches passing through the town each day. In addition a large number of long distance carriers regularly called at Stamford. Local carriers who travelled to and from nearby towns and villages added to this volume of traffic.

The growth in coaching meant an increase in the need for stabling and accommodation, and thus an increase in coaching inns. Existing inns such as the *George*, the *George and Angel* and the *Bull* adapted to meet the new trade. The frontage of the *George* was completely rebuilt by the Cecils in 1724. In that same year, Defoe stopped at the *George* 'out of curiosity because it is reckoned one of the greatest Inns in England'. A number of other inns can be dated to this period including the

Bull and Swan (then the *Falcon and Woolpack*) and the *Coach and Horses*, both in St Martin's.

Stamford's revival was not just down to the coaching trade. In 1664, Daniel Wigmore, a woollen draper, undertook the reconstruction of the canal; he succeeded where others had failed and reaped the rewards by collecting the tolls. As the Welland once again became navigable to the eastern ports it became possible to transport both the local barley crop and the malt produced in the town. This provided the stimulus for a thriving malting industry and, in 1676, the Cecils built a new wharf off Water Street to cope with the trade. Cargoes of stone and slates from Ketton and Collweston quarries, together with malt and agricultural produce, went downstream, with sea coal, timber and groceries being brought in on the inward journey.

Proposals were made in 1786 to connect Stamford with the Oakham canal and this was still the main issue at the 1809 election. However, a rival proposal for a canal from Stamford to Market Harborough caused a clash of interests and, in the event, neither proposal was put into practice.

With easy access to the river, Water Street became the centre of Stamford's malting trade, and by the late 18th century malting had diversified into brewing. A brewery was established behind no. 15 Water Street in 1780 and was bought by Joseph Phillips in 1789. It remained in the hands of the Phillips family until its closure in 1952. Hunts brewery opened in the same street in 1814 and continued successfully until 1927. All Saints brewery was started by William Edwards in 1825 and was purchased by Herbert Wells Melbourne and his brother in 1870. Although All Saints brewery closed in 1974, it remains as a brewery museum providing a continuing link with an important part of the town's commercial past.

In the 18th century England was first referred to as a 'nation of shopkeepers' and Stamford certainly reflected this. The general upturn in trade gave rise to the development

50 Portrait of the Rev. William Stukeley, rector of All Saints' and antiquarian.

of shops as we know them today, and to an increase in service industries. Market stalls were still to be found in High Street and Red Lion Square, and the shambles was still outside St Michael's. Now many more shops were opening, selling a much wider range of goods. From adverts in the *Stamford Mercury* we have a good idea of the range of household and luxury goods available. All sorts of fine tea, coffee, chocolates, castile soap, scented powder, ceramics, cutlery ware, medicines, silks, rich damasks, French brandy, wines, Delft ware and glassware were on offer. It was to Stamford that the region also turned for its professional services. The town's banks such as Eaton, Cayley and Co. provided business credit and, on occasion, assistance in setting up businesses. The land market was managed by Stamford lawyers who acted as stewards and agents to the neighbouring estates. Insurance agents also set up in the town.

As a town serving the local area, Stamford was also full of what we would now call specialist shops. There were cabinet makers, gunsmiths, brush makers, watch and clock makers, silver smiths and apothecaries, to name but a few. The fairs that had begun in the Middle Ages were still an important feature of the town's economy. By 1714 the town was holding six fairs and four large cattle markets each year.

Stamford Mercury:

BEING
HISTORICAL and POLITICAL
OBSERVATIONS
ON THE
Tranſactions of Europe.
TOGETHER WITH
Remarks on TRADE.

Thurſday, November 14 1717.

VOL. X. No. 19.

Printed by Tho. Baily and Will. Thompſon, at
Stamford in Lincolnſhire, 1717.

Price Three Half-pence.

Progress in agriculture provided additional stimulus. Small farms were being consolidated into much larger undertakings, and fen drainage and enclosure brought more land under cultivation. Increased crop production and improved stock breeding meant that local market centres such as Stamford benefited from the increased sale of produce in its shops and markets.

The town was rapidly developing as a trading centre for the region. As a result of this new-found prosperity, the town began to equip itself not only with new houses and shops but also with the public buildings and amenities of a social centre, attracting the rural elite from Leicestershire, Rutland and North-amptonshire. Polite society needed places to meet. The main meeting-places were the theatre, coffee houses and Assembly Rooms. Assemblies had been held at a house in Barn Hill from at least 1720. In 1727 these moved to the Assembly Rooms which had been opened by Askew Kirk as a dancing academy; card and tea rooms were added later in the century. The Assembly Rooms then, as now, became the venue for concerts and recitals. A subscription library was also opened in the town. Billiard tables were also available and a bowling green was opened where Rutland Terrace now stands. From 1714 (possibly from 1710) the town could boast its own news-paper, the *Stamford Mercury* which was published every market day.

51 *Stamford Mercury*, 1717. There is some debate about the exact date of the *Mercury*'s foundation. The paper still proclaims to have been established in 1695 although a date of 1710 or 1712 seems more likely.

52 A portrait of the Rev. Francis Peck, born in Stamford in 1692 and sometime curate of King's Cliffe and rector of Godeby. He was the author of the *Antiquarian Annals of Stanford,* published in 1727. This portrait was used as the frontispiece of Peck's *Memoirs of the Life and Actions of Oliver Cromwell,* published in 1740.

There appears to have been professional drama in the town before the building of the theatre in 1768. For example, the *Mercury* of 18 September 1718 announced that: 'Mr Kerrigan's company of comedians will be at the Guild Hall in Stamford, Lincolnshire during the time of the horse races, where will be acted comedies etc with several new and diverting entertainments.'

This performance was given in the guildhall, but there appears to have been an earlier theatre building. The *Mercury*, for example, refers to a theatre before 1768 and Burton, in describing the present theatre, talks of it having replaced an earlier theatre. The present theatre was opened in March 1768. The *Mercury* reported: 'On Monday last the New Theatre was opened here by Mr Whitley's Company of Comedians, with the comic opera of Love in a Village, which was performed much to the pleasure and satisfaction of a very numerous and polite audience.'

Stamford theatre is thought to be one of the earliest provincial theatres. In 1871 it closed and for a time became a billiard club. For some years the future of the building looked in doubt, but in 1977 it was completely refurbished, and in March 1978 it was reopened as a theatre.

Race week was the most important event on the social calendar, particularly after 1717 when the event was found a permanent home to the south of the town. Early in the 18th century races were held on Tuesday, Wednesday and Thursday in the second week in June. These meetings were well attended by the local aristocracy and townsfolk alike. In 1766 a grandstand was built which commanded a magnificent view of the course and surrounding countryside. The course itself was used for purposes other than racing. Cricket matches and sports meetings were held there and, on occasion, military reviews. In May 1772 The Royal Regiment of Horse Guards commanded by General Conway was reviewed on the race-course by General Pitt. The last race meeting was held there on 22 July 1873.

53 There was professional drama in Stamford as early as 1718 with notices of performances appearing regularly in the *Stamford Mercury*. The new theatre, or the Theatre Royal as it became known, was completed in 1768 and is reputed to be one of the earliest provincial theatres in the country. In 1871 it closed and became the Stamford Chess, Billiards and News Club. It was refurbished and re-opened as a theatre in 1978.

54 The Assembly Rooms in Stamford were amongst the earliest in the country. They were built by Askew Kirk, a dancing master, in 1727.

55 Daniel Lambert died whilst staying at the *Wagon and Horses* inn on 21 June 1809. He weighed almost 53 stone (336 kg) and measured 3ft. 11in. around the leg and 9ft. 4in. around the waist.

It was during race week in June 1809 that Daniel Lambert died. Lambert was not, as is often commonly thought, a native of Stamford, but came from Leicester. He arrived in Stamford from Huntingdon during the early part of race week and put up at the *Waggon and Horses* in St Martin's, intending to be available for the curious who might wish to call upon him. However, on 21 June 1809 he died. In his 40th year, he weighed 52st. 11lbs. and was only with great difficulty transferred in an immense elm coffin to the burial ground behind St Martin's Church.

Fox hunting, bowls, cockfighting, cards and bull running were all occasions which catered for the varying interests and social needs of the local and surrounding people of all classes. A number of cockpits in Stamford was in continual use during race weeks and at other times. The *George*, *White Swan*, *Red Lion*, *Half Moon* and *Roebuck* inns became the principal venues for cockfighting. The cockpit at the *George Inn* was built in 1725 by the 8th Earl of Exeter. An octagonal stone building, with an arched roof 40 feet in diameter, it was said to accommodate between 400 and 500

56 In April 1863 the Welland navigation was used for the last time, the canal having fallen into disrepair. Little remains to show the importance of the canal to Stamford's trade other than these warehouses (built 1756) which stand at the west end of Wharf Road.

57 Holkings, Tailor & Hatter, Broad Street. A good example of a mid-18th-century shop.

58 No. 3 All Saints' Place has been described as one of the finest Georgian houses in the town. Built in 1716, the house was used as the home of the Lydgates in the filming of the BBC's adaptation of *Middlemarch*.

spectators, and stood across what is now Station Road facing the Burghley almshouses. This cockpit is clearly shown on Knipe's map of 1833. There was also another cockpit in the *Stamford Hotel* yard, almost where the rear of the Woolworth extension now is. For the lower classes, the annual bull-run held in November (and occasionally at other times) matched the race meetings of the more well-to-do.

The pattern of building in Stamford shows that the middle classes favoured certain areas of the town. Thus, St George's Square, Barn Hill and High Street St Martin's stand out as enclaves of the better-off. In the 1780s the sheep market was moved from Barn Hill to a new site near the castle. Clearly a market on the doorstep was not in keeping with the new-found status of the residents of Barn Hill. In all this, however, social distinctions began to become more pronounced and many of the slums that disfigured the town in the 19th and early 20th centuries began to appear.

Whilst the town was generally becoming more affluent, there was little improvement in the condition of the poor of the town. Most parishes provided poor relief through the out-payments system and this was becoming an increasingly heavy expense, not only in Stamford but in just about every other parish in the country. In 1700 Thomas Trusedale, a wealthy lawyer, endowed an almshouse in Scotgate to house six poor men; and in 1763 George Williamson, a grocer, set up a small almshouse in St Peter's Street. Much later, in 1770, the Corporation gave land near St Peter's gate on which the mayor, John Hopkins, built an almshouse for poor married couples. In the interests of better health, four doctors opened a public bath house in 1722. The corporation were forced to address the problem of poverty within the town and, in 1739, converted Brazenose House (adjacent to the present Brazenose House) in St Paul's Street into a workhouse. This appears to have been funded jointly by the parishes of All Saints, St John, St George and St Michael. By 1801 only St Michael's was still supporting the workhouse, all the other parishes having left the scheme to set up small workhouses in their own parishes. The corporation also built 16 back-to-back houses in Scotgate (Corporation Buildings) to rent cheaply to the poor.

There were also concerns about the lack of education amongst the poorer people of the town and, in 1704, the Corporation founded the Bluecoat School. Originally known as the Charity School, it quickly became known as the Spinning School as one of its objectives was to teach the pupils to spin; it became known as the Bluecoat School from about the middle of the 18th century. Interestingly, the corporation only supported the School to the extent of £20 a year for three years, after which its future depended on the charitable impulses of others.

59 No. 41 High Street dates from the middle of the 18th century, with the shop front being added in the early 19th century. The site was acquired by the Peterborough Co-operative Society in 1901 and the shop was demolished in 1909 to make way for the present Co-op building.

60   Since the Middle Ages a room over the gateway on the bridge had served as the town hall. However, by the 18th century the gate had become an impediment to the increased traffic using the bridge. The Trustees of the Wansford Turnpike approached the Corporation in 1774 about re-siting the town hall so that the gate could be demolished. The new Town Hall was built on the site of the Monday market at the corner of St Mary's Hill and St Mary's Place. It was completed in 1779.

61   Behind the Town Hall was the Borough Gaol and House of Correction which were built in 1821 and rebuilt in 1824. The treadmill was just one of many ways in which the inmates were put to work. The gaol closed in 1878 and was pulled down in 1903.

Within five years of Robert Raikes founding the Sunday Schools movement in 1780, such schools were set up by the main churches in the town, to help educate the poorer children.

As Martin Smith has rightly pointed out in *The Story of Stamford*, 'the established church found itself being alienated from the poor'. This gave added impetus to the growth of nonconformity in the town. Following the Act of Uniformity of 1662, a large number of Church of England clergy were ejected from their livings, among them Mr Richardson, rector of St Michael's, who, under the terms of the Five Mile Act, had to leave town and reside in Uppingham. It is probably due to men like him that, after the Indulgence of 1672, an Independent chapel was erected in the town. This chapel was fairly short-lived because in 1714 it was destroyed by a Jacobite mob. In 1720 a new chapel was erected capable of sitting 300 people, which suggests that the nonconformists had a fairly large following by that time.

Whilst there were many worthy priests within the established church, there were some who seem to have spent more time pursuing

62 The portico was designed by William Legg and opened in 1808. Legg's design was based on St Paul's Church, Covent Garden, London.

63 The United Reformed church, Star Lane, formerly the Congregational chapel. This stands on land purchased in 1719 following the destruction in 1714 of an earlier chapel in St Paul's Street by a Jacobite mob. The present chapel was opened in September 1819 replacing that built in 1720.

their antiquarian interests than looking after their parishes. A central figure in local antiquarianism was the Rev. William Stukeley, Rector of All Saints'. In 1736 he founded a literary and antiquarian society in the town under the name of the Brazenose Society, prompted, one supposes, by neighbouring associations such as the Spalding Gentlemen's Society founded by Maurice Johnson in 1710, or the Peterborough Society started by the Rev. Timothy Neave in 1730. The Brazenose Society was not a success and very quickly faded away. Similarly the Clergyman's Book Club, which he also started, 'proved absolutely abortive: for they had no taste for anything but wine and tobacco'. The Rev. Francis Peck, a native of Stamford, was for a time curate at Kings Cliffe and then rector of Godeby Marwood. Like Stukeley, Peck was another Stamford antiquarian who, in 1727, published his *Antiquarian Annals of Stanford*.

The inability of the Church of England to address social problems also did much to further the cause of Methodism. This movement, founded by John Wesley, used outdoor preaching (which was forbidden by the Church of England) as a means of reaching more people. The movement broke away from the Established Church in 1795 and, by 1804, there was sufficient local support for a Methodist chapel to be built in Barn Hill.

In the early years of the century the Cecil interest in the town was purely that of a major landholder. It moved beyond this in 1727 with an attack on the Bertie dominance in the parliamentary elections. This quarrel came to a head in 1737 when the Cecil's joined with the Noels (of Exton) to oust the Berties. Following a hard fought, and often violent, election, Cecil won the day. In 1747 Lord Exeter bought back the manor of Stamford from the earls of Stamford for just under £7,000. Thus the town settled down under what was described at the time as 'the overpowering weight of aristocratical influence'.

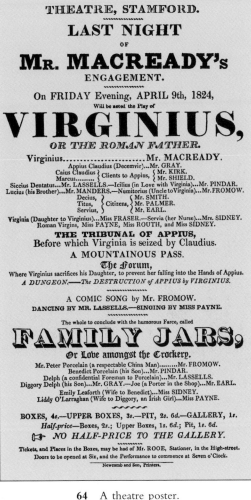

64 A theatre poster.

Stamford's modern street scene owes much to the grand designs of the 9th Earl of Exeter. In 1775-6, when the turnpike commissioners demanded the removal of the old Town Hall and gate from the north end of the bridge, the 9th Earl helped finance a new Town Hall on St Mary's Hill. In the 1770s the Earl began to redevelop the south side of St Mary's Street and the west side of St Mary's Hill. The resulting large, plain, three-storey terraces are somewhat out of keeping with some of the town's other 18th-century buildings, so it is probable that the design was dictated by the need for economy. The Earl was responsible

65   This shop in St Mary's Street was built in 1791-2 and was originally St John's Rectory. It became a shop in the early 19th century when the shop front with its two bow windows was added.

for the rebuilding of other properties in the town, and it appears that this work might have gone on indefinitely. However, on his death in 1793, his successor, the 10th Earl, brought the whole project to a speedy conclusion, only allowing the completion of work in hand.

At the end of the 18th century Stamford had the overall appearance of a busy town, helped by the Great North Road; it was said to be much busier than Lincoln. There was no industry on any large scale. Instead, the town had become firmly established as a social centre. The character of the town is reflected in the types of services offered. Apart from a large number of builders, plumbers, glaziers and painters there were gardeners and seedsmen; pipe makers, perfumeries, coachmen, booksellers, printers, stationers, writing masters, dancing masters and a significant number of apothecaries. Other commodities were supplied by confectioners, gingerbread makers, ribbon weavers, milliners and drapers. The town also boasted an impressive number of private boarding and day schools which had been set up to meet the educational needs of middle-class children.

Eight

ROTTEN BOROUGH

STAMFORD GREW VERY LITTLE during the 19th century; in fact, its growth was quite deliberately restricted. The reasons for this lay in the need of the 2nd Marquess of Exeter to preserve his political monopoly in the town. Nationally, however, things were changing and beginning to threaten the old order. Britain in the 18th and early 19th centuries might, like many European states, claim to have a government based on representation in parliament, but the representation was of interests rather than people. For many hundreds of years this had been based on the agricultural and property interests of the great landowners, and their paternalistic attitude to their tenants and employees. This was supported in no small measure by local shopkeepers and tradesmen who depended on the patronage of families such as the Cecils for a considerable part of their business. However, industrialisation and growing radicalism, based on ideas of equality and electoral reform, threatened the very stability of institutions like the Cecil estate. Lord Exeter, therefore, was implacably against any measure of reform or indeed anything that affected the status quo.

Until 1698 the town was variously represented in parliament by members of the local aristocracy or squirarchy. These included the Berties, Hatchers, Wingfield and Custs. After 1698 the influence of John, 5th Earl of Exeter began to bear sway in the town. It was in that year that William Cecil (a younger son of the 5th Earl) was elected alongside Charles Bertie.

From then on, until 1727, one Cecil and one Bertie (or Noel) always shared the two seats. The Cecil and Cust families were opposed to each other until 1734, when the decisive political battle was fought and won by what became known as the Cecil/Noel confederacy. Thereafter, with only two exceptions between 1734 and 1874 (when the borough was disfranchised), all members of parliament for Stamford were nominated by the earls or marquesses of Exeter. Furthermore, between 1734 and 1809, a period of 75 years, and between 1847 and 1874 (27 years) there were no election contests in the town. In the whole of the 19th century only ten contests were fought and in only eight cases did the voters actually go to the poll.

So, what type of political culture prevailed during the 18th and 19th centuries? Stamford was a prime example of what has become known as a Rotten or Pocket Borough. Old Sarum in Wiltshire and Castle Rising in Norfolk are other well known examples. In these boroughs not only were political practices suspect, but the number of MPs they returned was out of all proportion to the electorate. Many of the new industrial towns, such as Leeds, Manchester and Birmingham, had no MP at all; other large towns had only one. Stamford, with its fairly small population, had two until the second seat was removed by the second Reform Act of 1867.

Some Stamford elections were fought over particular issues. Such was the case in 1809 with the proposed Stamford to Oakham canal. Both nationally and locally, there was considerable hardship and depression following the end of the Napoleonic wars. Stamford's main industry at the time was malting and brewing and, in order to trade competitively, it was essential that Stamford became linked to the national canal network. The candidate put forward in opposition to the Exeter nominee was a London merchant, Joshua Jepson Oddy. He attracted the support not only of local bankers but also, somewhat unexpectedly, from Sir Gerard Noel of Exton. Oddy fought the election on mainly economic issues and was clear in his support for the Stamford to Oakham canal. It was probably not wise to highlight, as he did, the differing interests of the large landowners and those who earned their living through trade. Not surprisingly, the Exeter candidates won with a clear majority. This was the only election for which Oddy stood; he emerged as something of a dubious character who had been a bankrupt in the Fleet Prison. At the 1812 election Gerard Noel became the Whig candidate.

The secret ballot was not introduced until 1872. Therefore, those living in Exeter-owned properties, or dependent on the Estate for their job or their business, had little option but to vote for the Burghley candidate. To do otherwise was a certain path to eviction or unemployment. Shortly after the 1809 election some twenty of Exeter's tenants received notice to quit. A number of children were also refused admission to the Bluecoat School, their parents having voted for the 'wrong' candidate. In the 1830 election, at which Charles Tennyson stood for the first time, some thirty to forty tenants who voted against the Cecil interest were given notice to quit. Following this particular election, violent abuse was directed at Lord Exeter whenever he appeared in the town. Those who were evicted for voting according to their consciences had to be rehoused somewhere and there was little spare accommodation in the town. In a bid to solve this problem tenements were purchased

in various parts of Stamford. Following the 1809 election Oddy purchased a tenement in Scotgate (Protection Place) to house his homeless supporters and he also took a lease on Billings Buildings (High Street) for the same purpose.

Stamford's notoriety as a pocket borough was so great that it was frequently held up as an example of all that was corrupt in 19th-century politics. For example, the Tithe Commissioner wrote in 1839: '[Lord Exeter's control of Stamford is] a state of barbarous intervention and blindness, which resembles more an African domination than an English and wholesome interference'.

A report of the Reform League in 1868 was even more to the point:

> For past years Stamford has been a pocket borough belonging to the Marquess of Exeter, who lives close to the town and owns a great portion of it. There are no manufacturers in the place except a small firm who make agricultural implements, and the tradespeople depend on the surrounding gentry for their custom, so their [sic] is no independence in the place.

Writing as late as 1880, Gladstone referred to Stamford as a 'Tory fortress which has been used from time to time, to find accommodation for a wandering Tory official who had been rejected by some constituency that was weary of him'.

During the 1820s there was continued pressure for parliamentary reform. It was not until 1830 that the main obstacle to such reform was removed. The Tory party, which had consistently opposed any change in the constitution, lost its majority in the Commons for the first time in half a century. In Stamford this stimulated renewed interest in the Whig party and Richard Newcombe, the proprietor of the *Stamford Mercury*, was influential in his support. Newcombe formed an alliance with John Drakard, editor of the *Stamford News*, and invited Charles Tennyson to stand as candidate. There was clearly widespread support for reform and it was reported that 10,000 people greeted

Tennyson when he arrived in Stamford. This was probably something of an exaggeration since the total population of the town was only just over nine thousand. Tennyson addressed the crowd from the upper floor of the *George and Angel* in St Mary's Street, and such was his popularity that, for a time, the inn was renamed the *Tennyson Arms* in his honour.

In May 1831 the *Stamford Champion* reported that two Russian noblemen had been advised to go and observe the parliamentary elections held in that month because it would provide them with an illustration of the 'Greatest battle between the aristocracy and the people'.

They would certainly have had some excellent entertainment. For the first time since 1734, a candidate who opposed the Cecil interest was elected. This was despite the fact that the Marquess hired a gang of prize fighters to defend his candidates. On this occasion, Charles Tennyson (an uncle of Alfred, Lord Tennyson) was elected alongside Lord Thomas Cecil, Lord Exeter's brother.

Behind all this, of course, lay the power of the Cecils. The basis of this power was derived, in the first place, from land ownership. Within the immediate area of Stamford the family owned about 28,000 acres, and only ever sold land away from Stamford to pay debts etc. In addition, of course, the family owned a large proportion of the land and property in the town having bought back, from the Grey family, the manor of Stamford in 1747. Lord Exeter's overriding wish to retain control of the Borough's parliamentary seats lay in his need to preserve the aristocratic rights and privileges of a great landowner in the midst of a rising tide of Liberal thought and action. There had never been any serious opposition to the Cecils until the early 19th century when Whig opposition became more organised. In 1812 John Drakard's radical newspaper the *Stamford News* criticised the Cecils for their interference in local affairs. Much was also done by the Whigs to highlight corruption in the

town. Thomas Blore's investigations into the schools, hospitals and charities of the town, which he published in 1813, did a great deal to expose the degree of mis-management and fraud that existed within Stamford's institutions and charities.

The clergy of the town also had an important part to play in helping to preserve the Cecils' political monopoly, not so much for their own vote, though this was important, but for the influence they wielded in appointing the various parish officers. It became the policy of the Cecils to purchase the advowson (the right of presentation) of the parishes, so that Lord Exeter could appoint the town's clergy. The one place that held out against this was Browne's Hospital, for here Cecil could not obtain the right of presentation. In 1737-8 the mayor and Lord Exeter's agent together with a number of their supporters laid siege to the chapel of Browne's Hospital in an unsuccessful bid to induct the Burghley candidate as Confrator.

Opponents of the Cecils believed that the only way to challenge their influence was to create an estate in the town in which to house people who were not dependent on Lord Exeter. Sir Gerard Noel and Richard Newcombe both exhausted their resources in a vain attempt to do this. In 1810, Noel began building the *Stamford Hotel* which for a time became the political headquarters of the Whigs. However, following his defeat in the election of 1812, Noel appears to have abandoned the cause and the hotel stood empty until 1825 when it was bought by Thomas Standwell. Between 1839 and 1842 Richard Newcombe built Clock House, Rock Terrace and Rock House. Whatever the original intention, none of this building activity was likely to assist the poorer members of the electorate. Rock House was built for Newcombe's own use, and Clock House and Rock Terrace were clearly intended for middle-class tenants who could not necessarily be relied upon to support the Whig cause.

Before 1832 the Burghley estates outside Stamford were to prove politically useful. One of the many strategies employed by Exeter was to bring in tenants from outside the town, give them lodgings and enter their names on the list of voters as residents. Many of these were St Martin's men (St Martin's did not become part of the borough until 1832) who, traditionally, were detested by the inhabitants of the borough. This was done during the 1734 election, which proved to be so violent and corrupt that it brought to an end any further contest for the next 75 years. The poll on that occasion amounted to 520 voters, 113 more than in the previous election 'and more than there are houses in the town that can vote'.

Straightforward bribery also had a part to play in elections. According to Burton, a bonus of 5s. 3d. from each member used to be paid to each voter until 1820, when the Marquess of Exeter's steward paid two guineas to several electors for past services. More subtle forms of inducement were also employed. In the run-up to the 1830 election Tennyson gave a dinner at different public houses for some 600 people, and a ball in a large marquee which was erected in Broad Street, and the whole of the portico and the Shambles which about two thousand people attended. Voters and friends of the other candidates were also treated at various public houses in the town and free tickets were issued for performances at the theatre. This gave rise to a violent incident in September 1830 when a blue attempted to gain admission to the theatre and was refused admittance. A riot broke out and the doors of the theatre were thrown into the river. Generally, Stamford elections were 'dry' in the sense that the electors were not bribed with drink. However, in 1832 the Marquess of Exeter was rumoured to have spent £14,000 in an attempt to 'influence' the outcome of the election.

Although by the middle of the 19th century the population of the town had grown to just over 9,000, the number of parliamentary voters remained fairly small. At the beginning of the 18th century it was between 300 and 400, and by the early part of the 19th century it had risen to 800 voters. Between 1847 and the extension of the franchise in 1867 it was a mere 600. So who had the vote? The right to vote in parliamentary elections was obtained by paying Scot and Lot (payment made by town dwellers for the upkeep of the various borough facilities) and the poor rate.

The Boundary Act which accompanied the 1832 Reform Act added a large part of St Martin's to the borough of Stamford. This was largely Exeter territory and its inclusion in the borough would clearly be to Exeter's advantage in future elections. Charles Tennyson's view was that this change made it 'impossible for any independent candidate to survive against the Burghley interest', and declined to fight another election against such odds.

The franchise was extended three times in the 19th century by Acts we now refer to as the Three Reform Bills. The effect of the first Reform bill was to standardise the Urban franchise at £10 rental; in other words it limited the vote to householders rather than those who paid the poor rate. The irony of this was that, instead of weakening Exeter's hand, it actually strengthened it as it reduced the number of voters. There were 200 fewer in 1847 than in 1832 despite the fact that the population increased by about one thousand.

The shape of Stamford today is a direct result of the political battles of the 19th century. The majority of the electorate either lived in Cecil-owned houses or were dependent on the Cecils for their livelihood. For such people it was in their own best interests to vote for the Cecil candidate. The only way to get the better of this system was to build houses that were not owned by Cecil. This, however, was virtually impossible since there was no land on which to build. Exeter was well aware of this and steadfastly set himself against any attempt to enclose the open fields to the north of the town. Potentially about one thousand acres could have been given over to building and, although Lord Exeter owned the greater part of it, he had no option but to oppose enclosure.

Nine

GROWTH AND CHANGE

THE IMPETUS OF THE 18TH CENTURY continued well into the first half of the 19th century, with a good level of economic activity. Fairs and markets continued in the time-honoured tradition; the main fair was held in mid-Lent but others were held in February, May, June, August, and November. In 1821 newspapers reported an increase in the sales of wool, sheep and horses at Stamford fair. The town continued to serve a wide region as the focal point for trade and continued to do so despite the difficult years following the Napoleonic Wars.

In these early years of the century the increasing population, together with growing prosperity, led to an upsurge in civic pride and to a number of general improvements, particularly to buildings. In 1809 the portico in High Steet was built (now the public library) as the entrance to a new combined market. The white meat market in Red Lion Square and the Monday Market in St Mary's Place were both moved to the portico; this building also housed the fire engine, the town beadle and the police office. Some historians, however, see the move of the white meat market and the Monday market to the portico as a sign of their decline. The corn market, which had been established in 972, moved into a new arcaded hall in front of Browne's Hospital, the money being raised by public subscription. In 1819 the corn market was said to be the fourth largest outside London, although by the time the market moved in 1839 its business had considerably reduced. A new

Corn Exchange was built in 1859, but this was too big for the size of the market by that date. The cattle market remained in Broad Street until the end of the century. When in 1832 St Michael's Church collapsed, there was sufficient wealth in the town to ensure that it was completely rebuilt in the Early English Gothic style. It was enthusiastically described by the *Stamford Mercury* as 'one of the most beautiful buildings in the Kingdom'.

Some improvements were of more benefit to the whole community. A public subscription was opened for a gas works and this was built during 1824-5 on the old tenter meadow in Wharf Road. Now, for the first time, streets, public buildings and houses could be properly lit. The Stamford Improvement Act of 1841, amongst other things, allowed the formation of a private fire brigade. This brigade, which came to be dominated by the Gibson family, served the town until the formation of the Stamford Volunteer Fire Brigade in 1888.

The Stamford Scientific and Literary Institute was founded in 1838 'for the dissemination of literary, philosophical, scientific, mechanical and other useful knowledge'. The 'Institution', as it became known, quickly outgrew its original Broad Street premises and in 1842 commissioned a new building in the Greco-Egyptian style on St Peter's Hill. Cecil patronage of the Institution gave it something of an upper-class ethos as a result of which a rival Mechanics' Institute was established, which held its first meeting in 1841.

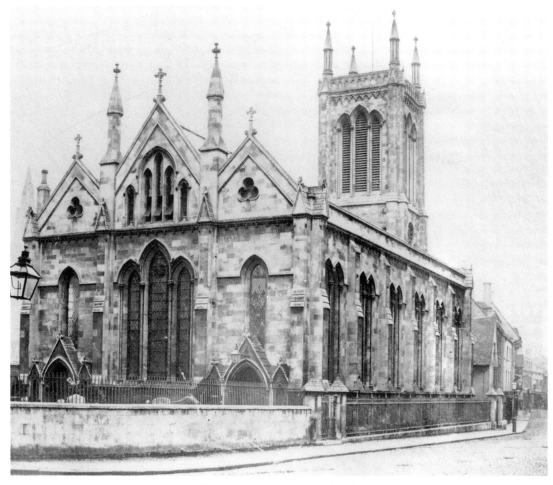

66 During alterations in 1832, the medieval church of St Michael collapsed. The damage was such that it was decided that total replacement was the only option. The designer was John Brown and the foundation stone was laid on 12 May 1835. The church was opened on 19 October 1836.

67 Henry Fryer, surgeon, in his will of 1823 bequeathed a large sum of money for an infirmary, providing it was built within five years of his death. The organising committee invited designs for the new hospital. A Gothic design submitted by J.P. Gandy was the final choice and the hospital opened in 1828.

The 19th century saw a significant increase in the number of private schools in the town. Records show that in 1842 there were no fewer than 22 schools and academies in the town, many of them in the St Paul's Street and Barn Hill areas. Several theories have been put forward for this increase in the number of schools, including the reflected glory of the Brazenose secession of the 1330s. However, it seems more likely that the town's position on the Great North Road made it an ideal location for the provision of boarding schools for the area. Schooling for working-class children continued to be provided by the Bluecoat, St Martin's and All Saints schools and, in 1815, the Girls National School was opened in Wharf Road. Later this became St George's School. An infants school was opened in the old cholera house in North Street in 1833, and by 1837 was said to have 110 pupils. St Michael's parish opened a school in about 1855 to be followed by the opening of St John's School in 1861.

In 1823 local surgeon Henry Fryer bequeathed the sum of £7,477 for the founding of an infirmary, providing it was built within five years of his death. The infirmary was duly built and opened on 5 August 1828. A number of architects were invited to submit designs for 'A building to contain not less than 20 patients and be capable of conveniently accommodating 32 if necessary'. It was also rumoured at the time that the architects were given instructions to design the building in such a way that, if the charity failed, it could easily be turned into a private house. There may be some truth in this since, if one views the building from the front and ignores the modern extensions, it very much resembles a large country house. The architect finally chosen for the project was a J.P. Gandy. In 1844 a fever ward was added to the original building.

Although treatment in the hospital was free, the process of gaining admission as a patient was not easy. Prospective patients needed a nomination from a subscriber to the charity in order to be admitted. Subscribers to the hospital charity were able to nominate in- or out-patients according to the level of their personal

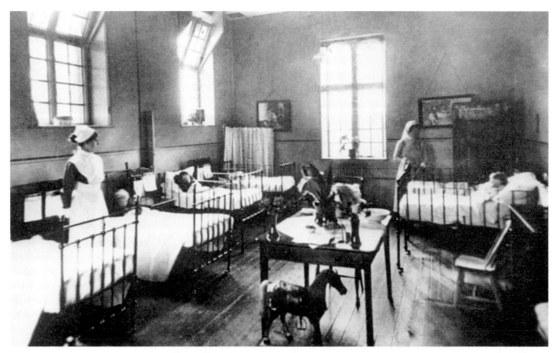

68   Stamford hospital, children's ward. This photograph is thought to date from the 1920s.

69   Trusedale's Hospital. Designed by George Basevi and built in 1832.

contribution. For example, subscribers of one guinea a year would be entitled to recommend two out-patients a year. This system survived until the foundation of the National Health Service in 1948. Many older Stamfordians can still remember being ill as children and their parents having to find a subscriber so that they could be admitted to hospital.

Until the early 1840s coaching was still the backbone of Stamford's prosperity, but the days of long-distance coaching were numbered with the coming of the railways. Even before Stamford had its own railway station, it became involved in railway controversy. In June 1846 Parliament sanctioned the building of the Great Northern Railway from London to York. Two years before this, in 1844, there had been a meeting at the *Stamford Hotel*, which was attended by George Stephenson, to discuss the Great Northern Railway and the possibility of routing it through Stamford. However, it was eventually decided to take the line through Peterborough. The reasons for the line avoiding

Stamford have always been hotly debated and the 2nd Marquess of Exeter has usually been held accountable for preventing the line from coming to the town. However, the truth of the matter was explained by Sir James Buller East in reply to a Parliamentary question raised by the Marquis of Granby on 8 June 1848: it was true that the Marquess of Exeter had objected to the proposal, but the simple fact was that the line to the north had to be as short and straight as possible. Therefore, it made no sense to divert it through Stamford. This was not the first, or the last, time that Stamford lost out to the interests of others. However, in this case we should perhaps be grateful that Stamford's integrity was maintained and that it was Peterborough which expanded to meet the needs of the railways.

It was decided that Stamford's interests could best be served by the Syston-Peterborough Railway and work began on the line in 1845, although it would be three years before it was finally finished, much of the delay

70 The *Stamford Hotel* was one of the grandest Regency hotels in the country. It was designed by John Linnell Bond for Sir Gerard Noel of Exton. As well as being an hotel it was intended to serve as the political headquarters of the Whig party.

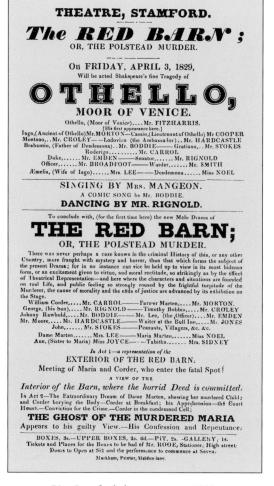

71   Stamford theatre poster, 1829.

72   The new town bridge was finally completed in 1849. As a means of helping to defray the cost, tolls were levied on all traffic crossing the bridge.

being caused by engineering difficulties on the western section and problems in Stapleford Park. However, in July 1846 a temporary station was built at the end of Water Street on the site of the future Great Northern station. The line between Stamford and Peterborough was finally opened on 2 October 1846. At this time there was still no line westwards from Stamford. The SPR contractors finally reached Stamford and in March 1847 began excavating the tunnel under St Martin's. Five months later this was still going on, and it is reported that during blasting operations many nearby houses had their roofs damaged by falling stones weighing up to twelve pounds. The Syston-Peterborough line was completed in 1848.

In 1847, when the Peterborough-Ely railway opened, it was possible to go from Stamford to London via Cambridge for a single fare of 15s. first class, 10s. second class and 6s. third class.

When the GNR opened in 1852 a regular omnibus service was started from the *Stamford Hotel* to Tallington station, to connect with trains to both London and York.

The final stage of railway development in the area came with the formation of the Stamford & Essendine Railway. In November 1852 the *Stamford Mercury* reported that:

> Among the parliamentary papers which will be found in our column today is one for an Act to authorise the construction of a railway from Stamford to Essendine. It will connect the Midland line with the Great Northern and will prove a most important branch for the inhabitants of Stamford.

This project, which had the full support of the Marquess of Exeter, was built to connect Stamford with the GNR at Essendine. Despite some initial opposition from the Midland Railway, work began on the new line in 1854 and it was opened in November 1856. The station for the S. & E. Railway, which became known as Stamford East, was built at the end of Water Street using the site of the Midland Railway's earlier temporary station. During

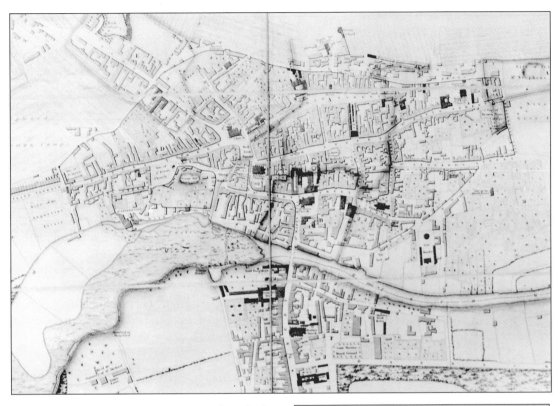

73 Detail from James Knipe's 1833 map of Stamford.

THE Public are most respectfully informed that the YORK HIGHFLYER COACH will leave the RED LION INN, GRANTHAM, at a Quarter before Seven every Morning, and arrive at the WHITE HORSE, *Fetter-lane*, LONDON, at a Quarter before Eight in the Evening—doing the 110 miles in 13 hours.

N. B. This Coach reaches Grantham at a Quarter past Six, stopping half an hour for Breakfast.

SLEAFORD, STAMFORD, CAMBRIDGE, LONDON' LEICESTER, and BIRMINGHAM DAY COACH, *Called THE AGE.*

THE inhabitants of SLEAFORD, FALKINGHAM, and BOURN, and the public in general, are respectfully informed that, for their better accommodation, a new COACH called THE AGE has commenced running from Sleaford to Stamford, from whence Passengers and Parcels are forwarded to Cambridge, London, Leicester, and Birmingham, and will arrive at those places the same evening certain.

The Age will leave Sleaford every Monday, Wednesday, and Friday Mornings, at Eight o'clock, Falkingham at Nine, Bourn at Ten, and arrive at Stamford by Eleven; return from Stamford every Tuesday, Thursday, and Saturday Afternoon, at Five o'clock, after the arrival of Coaches from the above places, and will reach Bourn at Six, Falkingham at Seven, and Sleaford at Eight o'clock the same evening.—Performed by

WHINCUP and CO., Stamford.

74 One of the many coaching adverts to be found in the *Stamford Mercury*.

75 Lumby's Terrace originally consisted of two rows of houses. The terrace itself, the two houses at the north entrance and the two free-standing houses to the south were all built by Moses Lumby, a butcher. The dates of construction vary, but the row that remains is of about 1840.

the Second World War Stamford was designated a collection and dispersal centre for materials used in the war effort. This meant considerable additional work for the railways and Stamford East effectively became a goods depot, handling high volumes of freight. The Stamford & Essendine line finally closed on 2 March 1957.

The Welland Navigation, in common with other canals, was also hit hard by the coming of the railway. Plans to connect the Stamford canal to the wider canal network came to nothing but, in the light of rapid railway expansion and the general decline in the

waterways, this may have been no bad thing. The canal was last used for commercial purposes in 1863 by which time it was in a bad state, with water escaping into the river and most of the locks in need of repair.

The passing of the coaching trade clearly had a significant effect on the service industry; old coaching inns such as the *George and Angel* and the *Coach and Horses* were forced to close, and many others had to look elsewhere for their business. There seems to have been no shortage of business for the licensed trade; by the early 1850s the town was still supporting some 63 inns, 10 beer houses together with a number of unlicensed beer sellers.

The Industrial Revolution that turned many small towns into sprawling conurbations left Stamford largely untouched. But, true to its role as a market centre, such industry as did emerge had its beginnings in the needs of agriculture. Thomas Gibson opened his agricultural implement business at the junction of Broad Street and Star Lane in 1843. From small beginnings this firm grew to become a busy iron foundry and continued on its original site until closure in 1972. In 1845 the Cecils built an iron foundry on Wharf Road for J.C. Grant who produced a range of agricultural implements. However, this firm closed in 1851 when Grant suddenly died.

Despite the passing of coaching, Hayes and Sons, carriage and wagon builders founded in 1825, continued to prosper and became a major concern. By the 1880s they were turning out some three hundred new carts and coaches each year.

Blackstone's, which in the 20th century came to enjoy an international reputation as a maker of diesel engines, began life in 1837 in a small workshop in Sheepmarket. Founded by Henry Smith, the company began by making machinery for the agricultural market. In 1842 it moved to St Peter's Street, building another foundry where it continued to manufacture agricultural equipment. From 1846 all work was being undertaken at the Rutland Iron Works.

76 Rock Terrace, Scotgate, built in 1841 by Richard Newcombe as part of his plan to develop an estate within the town.

77 Rock House, Scotgate, was built by Richard Newcombe in 1842.

78 Richard Newcombe's proposal for a new street leading from St Mary's Hill to High Street got no further than the first two shops which were built *c.*1849. This was formerly the site of the *George and Angel Inn*.

The move to engine manufacture appears to have taken place in 1853, when Thomas Ashby joined the company, and it began to produce portable steam engines. In 1855 the company expanded still further and took over premises at Tithe Yard, St Peter's Street.

In 1886 the company, then known as Jeffrey & Blackstone, obtained a 10-acre site off Ryhall Road where it started to produce the oil engines on which its continued success was built. During the First and Second World Wars the company's production was turned over to war work. At its height, the company was the town's biggest employer with over 500 workers.

Not all commercial enterprise was geared to agriculture. In Wharf Road was to be found the Blashfield Terra Cotta works. This was another Stamford-based firm that enjoyed an international reputation, in this case for the fine quality of its terracotta products. The

works opened in March 1859 when John Marriot Blashfield fired the first kiln in the presence of the Marchioness of Exeter and her family. By 1861 the company was employing a considerable workforce, many of whom were Italian. The company advertised as potters and manufacturers of terracotta chimney pots, balusters, vases, statues etc. It was wound-up in 1875. There are still examples of Blashfield's work to be found in the town, notably the front of 30 High Street and the *Scotgate* public house. The boat-house at Burghley is also by Blashfield.

During the 19th century Stamford's pre-occupation with bull-running was finally brought to an end. The origins of this barbarous practice are unknown, although local legend has it that it was started in the 13th century by Earl Warenne. Whatever its origins, bull-running was a sport that Stamfordians were attached to and a bull-run was staged each year on 13 November. Whilst bull-running was not unique to Stamford (the practice was carried on in a number of towns including Wisbech, Tutbury and Tetbury), it does appear to have lasted much longer here than anywhere else. In Tutbury, for example, it was suppressed in 1778. Local opinion was clearly beginning to turn against the practice, for in 1785 the *Stamford Mercury* reported:

> Monday last being our annual bull-running, the same was observed here with the usual celebrity—several men heated with liquor got tossed by the bull, and were most terribly hurt, while some others more sober had little better usage. What a pity it is so barbarous a custom is permitted to be continued, that has no good purpose to recommend it, but is kept as an orgy of drunkenness and idleness to the manifest injury of many poor families, even tho' the men escape bodily hurt.

But in 1819 John Drakard's *Stamford News* criticised the hypocrisy of the objectors when they themselves indulged in fox-hunting.

In the years 1788 to 1790 the corporation attempted to put down the sport and in each of the three years went as far as bringing in special constables and troops of dragoons in a bid to stop the practice. But despite these precautions the bull was still run. After this, opposition to the sport appears to have subsided. Bull-running, or at least the promise of a bull-run, played an important part in some elections. Parliamentary candidates used the promise of a bull to win over the poorer voters; in fact, in 1831 the Burghley candidate canvassed under a large flag with a painting of a bull.

By the early 1830s the practice was declining in popularity though there was still a vestige of support. In 1833 a group of people, mostly dissenters, tried to bring it to an end but this actually rekindled interest. In the same year the Society for the Prevention of Cruelty to Animals sent an observer to Stamford, but he received very rough treatment from those supporting the sport. It looked set to continue, but the run in 1836 marked the beginning of the end. In March 1837 legal action was taken against eight of the people said to have been involved in the previous November's bull-run. Amongst other things they were charged with riotous assembly and assaulting a representative of the Society for the Prevention of Cruelty to Animals.

The conviction of the eight had little effect and November 1837 saw another bull-run, even though 221 special constables had been sworn in to try to stop it! In 1838 a troop of the 14th Light Dragoons and a detachment of the Metropolitan Police were brought into the town. Even this did not stop determined bullards from having their sport. At the following quarter sessions a further four people were indicted for riotous assembly. By this stage, the bull-run has almost become a battle of wits between the bullards and the local authority. In 1839, notwithstanding the presence of a captain and 43 troopers of the 5th Dragoon Guards plus an inspector and 20 London policemen and the appointment of special constables, the bullards still contrived to get a bull into the town, although only for a very short time.

However, this was to be the very last time that a bull-run would take place. In November 1840 a public meeting at the Town Hall presented a petition to the mayor and magistrates in which they suggested that if the borough council would reconsider calling in

79 Stamford Town Station which was completed in June 1848. The weather vane carries the letters SPR for the Syston-Peterborough Railway. This photograph also shows the extent to which in-fill building has encroached on the old station yard.

troops and police, they themselves would undertook to stop bull-running. The reasons for this were financial. In 1838 it had cost £150 to bring in troops and police, and in 1839 it had cost almost £300. This cost had to be met by the borough ratepayers who clearly decided enough was enough.

As the century progressed, the population of the town steadily increased and the town became more and more congested. In 1801, there were 4,000 people living largely within the area of the original medieval walls. By the time of the 1851 census this number had increased to 9,066 inhabitants. Despite this increase the town expanded hardly at all due, as we have seen, to the failure to enclose the open fields. This inevitably led to a high degree of overcrowding and the 1851 census shows that there were many instances of compara-tively modest houses accommodating three or more families. Space was at a premium; the parish of St Michael's could not find anywhere to establish a school, so in its early years the school was held in the back room of the *Dolphin* inn, Broad Street. For local schoolchildren there was a certain cachet in this since, as a school

inspector reported, they used to boast about going to school at the *Dolphin*. The same inspector reported that the school room had to be given up on market days so that it could be used for eating and drinking. In 1834 the only site that could be found for the new Union Workhouse was an old quarry in Barnack Road which was purchased from the Cecils and cost a small fortune to infill. When John George de Merveilleux, a local doctor, built the Baptist chapel in the same year it was necessary to encroach on the unenclosed northern fields. By 1828 about 100 cottages had already encroached on this land and in 1845 there were 380 houses as well as the Baptist chapel. This area of Stamford was particularly unsavoury, home to thieves and prostitutes. It was unlikely to be cleaned up, however, as the town council and the Marquess of Exeter were unable to agree on the ownership of the land.

In the 1840s the Blackfriars Estate was laid out between the town and the Welland, but many plots were used as gardens by the owners of old houses within the medieval boundaries, so this did little to ease the housing problem. Rutland Terrace was built on the site

80 Stamford East (GNR) Station. The station was built to resemble an Elizabethan mansion in recognition of Lord Exeter's patronage. The GNR line was opened in 1856, but after it lost its contract to run the line it was taken over by the Stamford to Essendine Railway. The SER closed in 1959.

81 Waterfield House stood on the corner of Castle Dyke and Sheep market. The arrangement of the windows suggests that it is medieval in origin, with an open hall at the east end. For many years the house was occupied by the Waterfield family of saddlers. The building was demolished in 1885.

82 The Stamford Scientific and Literary Institution was designed by local architect Bryan Browning and built in 1824. The building contained a large concert and lecture hall, with museum gallery and library. On the roof was an octagonal observatory with *camera obscura*. This was removed in 1910.

of the old bowling green in 1829, providing fashionable middle-class housing but doing little to alleviate the overall shortage. The 1851 census shows us that there were more people living in the four dwellings that constituted Freeman's Cottages than there were in the whole of Rutland Terrace. As the town did not attract large-scale industry, there was no large-scale working-class housing. Bath Row and the lanes off St Mary's Street became congested with small shabby cottages. There was some attempt to provide cheap housing such as the 16 houses built in Exeter Court, St Peter's Street; The Exeter Estate built 36 houses for artisans between Castle Street and Bath Row on the model of Glasgow tenements (Cooch's Court). Other building projects failed completely. Richard Newcombe's death in 1851 meant that his grand design for a terrace of shops from the top of St Mary's Hill to High Street never got further than the first two shops.

There was to be no real solution to the problem of overcrowding until the last quarter of the century and this came about through a combination of changes to the electoral system and the financial problems of the Cecils. The

83 Rutland Terrace. In 1827 the bowling green and an adjoining paddock were purchased as building land by J.C. Wallis, a veterinary surgeon. Building of all 20 of the houses had begun in 1829 and appears to have been completed by 1831.

84 The *Horns and Blue Boar*, Broad Street, photographed in about 1860. The building on the extreme right of the picture is the *Dolphin Inn*.

Cecils' control of the borough was weakened in 1867 by the passing of the Second Reform Act, which removed one of the town's two MPs and increased the number of voters from about 850 to just over one thousand. Five years later, the introduction of the secret ballot made intimidation much more difficult and effectively removed Cecil's means of control. In these new circumstances, the 1869 election was the first to be contested since 1848. However, further changes were on the way. In 1884 the Franchise Act removed Stamford's remaining seat and put the town into a larger South Lincolnshire constituency, where the Cecils had far less influence.

One other factor brought even closer a solution to the open fields. The arrival of cheap corn from America brought on a crisis in the agricultural industry, and landowners such as the Cecils saw a significant drop in their income. This, together with the Marquess's personal financial difficulties, left the estate in much need of capital. As the Cecils owned some one thousand acres of the open fields, enclosure became an attractive proposition. The Enclosure Act went through Parliament in 1871, becoming effective in 1875. This opened the door to considerable development to the north of the town. Land was sold to the Stamford Freehold Land Association, which developed an estate bordered by King's Road and Queen Street. Local builder John Woolston developed an estate to the east of Recreation Ground Road. All of this, however, was essentially lower middle- and working-class housing. Larger middle-class houses were built along Casterton, Empingham and Tinwell Roads. Although this land was sold for development, Lord Exeter did make provision for a recreation ground in Hunt's Close, just behind the Baptist chapel. Interestingly, the open fields of St Martin's parish, which was largely owned by the Cecils, had been enclosed 76 years earlier in 1795.

By the end of the 19th century government generally recognised the appalling poverty and unhealthy living conditions of the poorer classes. At the same time scientific and techno-logical improvements went some way towards

85 The Roman Catholic church, designed in a 13th-century Gothic style by the London architect George Goldie. The church was opened in 1864.

86 St Peter's Callis, in the mid–1850s. This photograph shows the original callis before its demolition in 1862-3. The term 'callis' for a hospital or almshouse is a local one and may derive from Stamford's association with the medieval wool staple of Calais.

87 The Burghley boat house, built by J.M. Blashfield.

providing solutions. A report on 'the sanitary state of Stamford in 1870' reveals something of the town's condition. Somewhat surprisingly, the town was quite healthy given that only a few streets possessed sewers; the Welland, as it passed through the town, was described as 'a most offensive cesspool' and was still liable to frequent flooding. Water was supplied from wells in private houses, from the Exeter Estate water works and from 15 public pumps scattered around the town. In 1868 and 1869 there were severe outbreaks of typhoid due to polluted water supplies. In line with Government recommendations isolation wards were built at the hospital in 1879. Slowly, the town's drainage, sewerage and water systems were all renewed.

Stamford never really suffered from a lack of schools and because of this escaped the establishment of a Board School under Forster's Education Act of 1870. This Act also stipulated that schools should provide good basic education, although education was not made

88 St Michael's National School started life in the back room of the *Dolphin Inn*, Broad Street. In 1861 this new school was opened at the corner of Recreation Ground Road and East Street. When St Michael's School closed the buildings were used for a number of years by the Bluecoat School.

89 This advert by Hayes and Son gives some idea of the range of vehicles produced by the company.

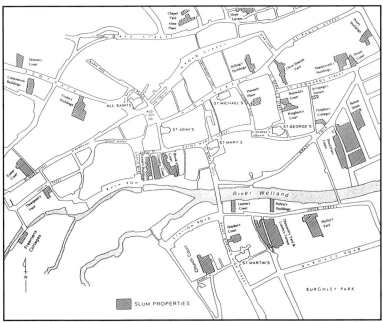

90 *Left*. Map showing the main slum areas in Stamford. The Blackfriars Estate was an area of small streets of slum tenements, including Belton Street, Gas Street, Milner's Row, Tenter Lane and Welland Street. In addition to these areas there were 70 to 80 individual tenements on the manorial waste to the north of the town. (Map based on that produced by the late Dr Eric Till.)

91 *Below left*. Laxton's Court, St Leonard's Street, drawn by Montague Jones.

92 *Below right*. Olive Branch Yard, St Leonard's Street. Drawing by Montague Jones.

93 *Above.* This panoramic view of Stamford from station yard shows the extent to which Bath Row was built on prior to the slum clearance programme.

94 *Right.* Stamford Grammar School was founded in 1532 by William Radcliffe, and was possibly using St Paul's Church as a schoolroom by 1548. The present buildings on the north side of St Paul's Street were built in 1874 under a scheme drawn up by the Endowed Schools Commissioners.

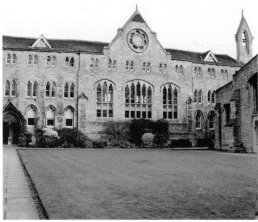

95 *Below.* Stamford High School for Girls, High Street, St Martin's. This school was opened in 1877 having been built under the same scheme that resulted in the rebuilding of the grammar school.

96 St Martin's School. This undated photograph shows the pupils and staff of the school. The gentleman in the top hat on the extreme right is Joseph Phillips. The man in the soft hat to the left of the doorway is Mr Knight, the headmaster.

compulsory until 1876. In Stamford money from Browne's Hospital and the Grammar School was used to establish a new elementary school which was situated in All Saints Street and became known as Browne's School. Provision was also made for senior schools for both boys and girls. The boys was based on the old Grammar School and the Girls High School was opened in High Street St Martin's in 1877.

As a borough Stamford for many hundreds of years enjoyed a degree of autonomy in its affairs. However, this was slowly coming to an end. In 1889 county councils were created and Stamford came under the authority of Kesteven County Council; this saw a significant reduction in the influence of the town council, as the

responsibility for decisions was vested outside Stamford.

Change became the order of the day. The Stamford police force, which had been formed in 1836, was soon disbanded. The Kesteven Council opened a Technical School in Broad Street (now the museum); the cattle market was removed from its time-honoured place in Broad Street to a new cattle market south of the river. Finally, in 1902 the workhouse which had stood in Barnack Road since 1836, was demolished and a new building was erected in Ryhall Road. This building, which became known as St George's Home, was itself demolished in 2001 to make way for retirement housing.

Ten

THE 20TH CENTURY AND INTO
THE NEW MILLENNIUM

THE ENCLOSURE ACT really came too late to make any significant difference to Stamford's industrial base. A description of the town, published in 1892, states: 'Taken as a whole, it seems doubtful whether Stamford will ever attain to any degree of industrial supremacy'. Even at this early date, the description suggests that the town runs a poor second to Peterborough or Grantham. However, despite this pessimism, there was sufficient work to see the population increase from 8,229 in 1901 to 9,647 by 1911. The

town's industry was varied but, in many cases, still geared to agriculture. An exception was the Pick Motor Company, although Pick did attempt to break into the tractor market.

A one-time employee of Blackstone's, Jack Pick went on to set up his own business and manufacture cars in the town. Ever the inventor, Pick left Blackstone's in 1895 and set up shop at the corner of St Leonard's Street and Brazenose Lane, where he manufactured a patent hoe that he had invented. In 1896 he went into partnership with A.J. Pledger as a

97 This triumphal arch was erected across High Street for the Stamford and Lincolnshire Agricultural Society Show of 1879.

98   Barn Hill Methodist church, built in 1886 to replace the earlier chapel of 1804.

99   Stamford Borough Police Force, photographed on the Town Hall steps, *c*.1884.

100   The presentation of long service medals to D Company 2nd V Battalion Lincolnshire Regiment in Red Lion Square, August 1895.

101   Photograph taken on the occasion of the last cattle market to be held in Broad Street, in 1896.

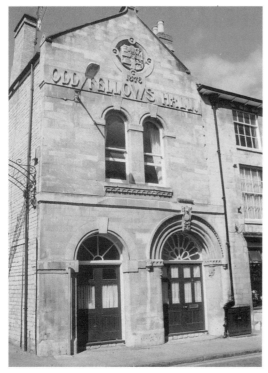

102 The Odd Fellows Hall was built in 1876 for the Albion Lodge. The hall was built on the site of Stamford's first Roman Catholic church.

103 John Woolston's post-enclosure building development in Recreation Ground Road.

cycle dealer and moved to premises at no. 5 Blackfriars Street. Under the title J.H. Pick and Co., he repaired and sold cycles as well as doing light engineering jobs and continuing with the production of hoes and needles. Business prospered, and in March 1899 Pick organised a two-day cycle show in the Assembly Rooms. Over a hundred bicycles with the latest improvements were on show. It was about this time that Pick built his first motor car. Having obtained an engine of 'French design' he installed it in a dogcart-style body. This car was sold to a Dr Benson of Market Deeping for £85. A second car was bought by the Marquess of Exeter.

Following this early success the Pick Motor Company Ltd was formed on 19 March 1900. The directors of the new company were the Marquess of Exeter and Sir George Whitcote, W. Bean Esq. of Wothorpe and Charles Gray, but not Pick who became works manager. This led to numerous disagreements between Pick and the directors in future years. Despite this, however, the firm did reasonably well and outgrew the Blackfriars Street site. A two-acre site was acquired between Blackfriars Steet and St Leonard's Street and a new factory was built. A *Stamford Mercury* reporter visited

104 Broad Street in 1900.

105 Stamford Fire Brigade. At the time this photograph was taken, the fire station was in East Street in the building which is now the St John Ambulance headquarters. The large silver cup is the Londesborough Cup which was won by the Stamford brigade for six years in succession and nine years in all, in North Eastern District competitions.

106 The mid-Lent Fair in Broad Street, *c*.1906.

107 Although the street scene has changed considerably, this is still clearly recognisable as St Mary's Street.

the factory soon after it opened in 1903 and wrote:

> Some fifty cars are at present in the course of construction, varying from 4½ to 24 horse power. The increasing importance of the manufactory to a town like Stamford, and the extent of the work turned out, may be gauged from the fact that the number of men employed at the commencement had grown to upwards of 100, and overtime had been general from the start.

However, all appears not to have gone well with Pick and his directors because late in 1904 advertisements were appearing in local papers for 'Pick's Motor Works, St Martin's, Stamford'. Just why Pick had left the Blackfriars works is not clear, but he set up his new business at 11 High Street St Martin's, opposite the *George Hotel*. For a time they took on just about any general engineering work they could get in order to tide them over. By 1906 a new chassis had been built, with a smart two-seater body built by Hayes and Son of Stamford mounted on it. This obviously proved something of a turning point since it became necessary to obtain extra production space and Pick took over the workshops vacated by Hayes and Son at the corner of High Street/ St Martin's and Barnack Road.

Motor-car production appears to have continued until 1915 when the works were turned over to war work. Unfortunately the works were not taken into government control which meant that, at the end of the war, the company was not eligible for subsidies or post-war assistance to replace machinery worn out by munitions production. This may be why Pick did not immediately return to car production. Whatever the reason, he missed out on the brief post-war demand for motors cars which led to a period of intense competition between car makers. Pick did approach

William Morris with a view to producing engines in Stamford. However, Morris turned him down on the quite reasonable grounds that he lacked the productive capacity. A brief venture into building tractors did little to restore the firm's fortunes. In 1923 Pick refinanced the company with the help of Charles Miles, a local timber merchant. This could have been a turning point for the company but, unfortunately, Pick's new design of car was not what the market wanted. He opted for a large 22 b.h.p. car with a slow revving engine at a time when Austin and Morris were producing small cars in response to the £1 per horse-power tax. Furthermore, the post-war boom quickly faded and depression set in. Demand for cars fell sharply, particularly for large cars. It is doubtful, therefore, whether Pick sold any of his new models. The firm finally went into voluntary liquidation in January 1925.

108 H.T. Betts, wine and spirit merchant, Broad Street. This business was well established by 1900. Although now in different hands, the shop is still a wine merchants—a good example of continuity of use of shops in Stamford. This photograph dates from c.1910.

109 Smedley's fish and game shop, High Street, *c*.1914.

110 St Martin's from Wharf Road. This is the site of the old ford which predates the town bridge. This photograph suggests that cattle were still being driven across in the early part of the 20th century.

111 Eel sellers outside Browne's Hospital. Mr and Mrs Robinson (extreme right and second from right) came regularly from Market Deeping to sell eels in Stamford. This photograph was taken *c.*1920.

112 In 1781 the sheep market was moved from the top of Barn Hill to the area that bears its name today. This photograph is probably of the St Simon and St Jude Fair (held in November) when stalls were set up in Castle Dyke, St Peter's Hill and into St Peter's Street.

113 To judge from this photograph, the mid-Lent Fair took up more of Red Lion Square in the early 20th century than it does today.

114 In 1913 Blackstone's built their Baroque-style showrooms in Broad Street. The building was sold in 1925 and converted into a cinema by the Cambridge Cinema Company. The building burned down in 1937 and was replaced by the present Art Deco building.

Locally Jack Pick has been favourably compared with William Morris. There are certainly parallels in the way their respective early careers developed. However, Morris was clearly the more astute businessman and succeeded where Pick failed. Had he not done so, Stamford may well have become another Cowley!

In the early 1900s the Williamson Cliff brickworks was developed to the north of the town on clay pits in Little Casterton Road. The hand-made facing bricks produced by the company gained an international reputation and were used extensively at colleges in both Oxford and Cambridge as they provided a good match for the older masonry in the buildings. In 1986 Stamford bricks were also used in building work at Buckingham Palace as well as for the more mundane purpose of paving the town's new pedestrian precinct in 1984.

At the end of the 19th century, a sharp fall in prices greatly increased the spending power of the working classes; in fact, between 1875 and 1900 prices had fallen by as much as 40 per cent. Working hours were also reduced. Records show that in 1890 workers at Blackstone's gained

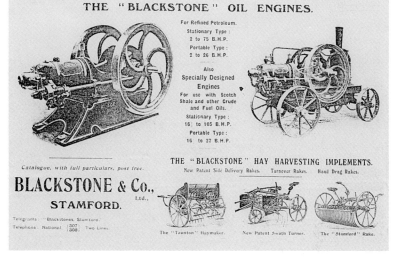

115 A general advertisement for the Blackstone oil engine, but also showing a range of agricultural equipment.

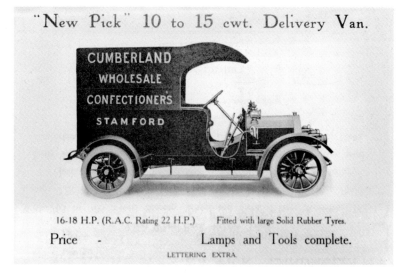

116 New Pick delivery van.

117   A general view of High Street in the 1920s.

118   High Street, St Martin's and the *George Hotel*. The shops above the Pick Motor works were demolished in the 1970s.

119 Looking along East Street from the corner of Recreation Ground Road. All of these buildings were scheduled for slum clearance in 1936 and for many years the site remained vacant until the Salvation Army Citadel was built in 1973.

120 Cooch's Court was built by the Exeter Estate. Intended for artisans, it was built on the model of a Glasgow tenement. This photograph was taken during the demolition of the site.

121 St George's Street. This scene gives a general impression of one of the town's 'poorer' areas in the early years of the 20th century. The house with the round chimney (No.11) is medieval in part and has been sadly neglected in recent years.

122 A view of High Street showing Grant's butcher's shop. This shop was removed in 1937 and is now in the Castle Museum, York.

a reduction in their working week to 62 hours! In 1893 the custom of shops closing early one day a week began. These small, but significant, steps meant that at the turn of the century people found themselves with more leisure time. This provided the impetus for a wide range of leisure activities. Stamford Football Club (The Daniels) was formed in 1896 and turned professional in 1910; a swimming pool was opened in 1913 while the public library had been opened in 1906. In 1885 Stamford Brass was formed and during the First World War its musical director was the 19-year-old Malcolm Sargent. The cinema always proved popular and the Picturedrome was opened in the Odd Fellows Hall in 1910. This was followed in 1913 by the Picture Palace in Blackfriars Street. The 'Electric Picturedrome' moved to Broad Street in 1927, next door to the Central Cinema which had been opened in 1926. The Central Cinema burned down in 1937 and was rebuilt by London architect George Coles in the Art Deco style. Malcolm Sargent's biography records that he attended the Picturedrome and that 'Sometimes on Saturday afternoons, he would sit by Harold Rudd at the piano and help 'fit' the films with music which they extemporised in part'.

At the outbreak of the First World War in August 1914 Stamford was gripped with that patriotic fervour that swept the rest of the country. Within the first year of the war some 1,700 (about 11 per cent) men from Stamford and district enlisted in the armed forces. As mobilisation got under way, troops were moved all over the country before leaving for France. Stamford found itself accommodating 600 men of the Essex Regiment as they completed their training and made final preparations for France. In 1915 the borough council invited a number of Belgian refugees to the town for the duration of the war. In the early part of the war the town's long association with the air force began with the opening of the airfields at Wittering and Easton. When the USA entered the war in 1917 trainee airmen were billeted in the town whilst they did their basic training at Wittering.

Stamford's firms were turned over to war work. The Kitson Empire Lighting Company (Wharf Road) made torpedo heads, Cuttings Electrical dynamos for the navy, Blackstone's shell casings and Hayes ammunition carts and wagons.

The inter-war years saw considerable changes in the town, born of the complex social consequences of the First World War. One of the priorities of Lloyd George's government was housing, and the Housing Act (1919) required certain uniform standards to be maintained and planned programmes of building to be put in place. Stamford's population was steadily increasing, putting considerable pressure on limited housing resources. At the end of the First World War there were over four hundred

123 Oates & Musson were one of Stamford's foremost shops for many years. This advertisement gives some idea of the range of goods and services available.

124 The new workhouse in Ryhall Road. This building was opened in 1902 to replace the workhouse built in 1836 in Barnack Road. It later became the St George's Home for the Elderly. The building was demolished in 2001 to make way for new retirement housing.

125 Council housing in Melbourne Road, where the council began its pre-war council-housing programme.

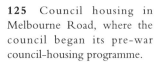

126 The Stamford Spitfire.

MUNDELLA SCHOOL - STAMFORD

EVACUATION RULES

A. OUT-OF-DOORS

1. Orderly behaviour is expected at all times.
2. School Uniform must be worn on week days.
3. All pupils must be in their billets within three quarters of an hour after the beginning of 'black-out' time. Permission to be out after this hour, may however, be granted to pupils who wish to attend approved activities.
4. Gas masks must be carried at all times, preferably in a waterproof container. The container must be labelled with the pupil's full name, school, evacuation address and National Registration number.
5. National Registration cards should be left in the charge of the host.
6. Bathing in the river is forbidden.
7. Cycling is permitted providing that a written application is made by the parents.
8. The small wood opposite the Fane School is out-of-bounds.
9. Prefects may exercise authority over other pupils out of school hours.
10. Identification labels must be worn at all times.
11. Great care must be taken in crossing the streets - especially those of the Great North Road.
12. Billeting changes must be reported at once to Mr. Adamson and the billeting teachers concerned.
13. Accidents to boys must be reported to Mr. Thorpe or Mr. Fletcher.
14. Accidents to girls must be reported to Miss Blagg, Miss Berry or Miss Waters.
15. Pupils are allowed to go home for week-ends provided that:-
(a) Parents send a written application at least one week beforehand.
(b) Parents sign the Parent's Responsibility Form.
(c) Application is made only once a month - emergencies excepted.
(d) Pupils leave after School on Fridays and report for School on Monday afternoons.

B. IN-DOORS

1. Pupils must be courteous and obedient to their hosts.
2. Pupils are expected to accompany their hosts to Church or to Chapel on Sundays if they are of the same denomination.
3. Pupils must be punctual for meals.
4. Great care must be taken to observe 'black-out' regulations.
5. Personal cleanliness is expected at all times.
6. Pupils should write home at least once a week.
7. All articles of clothing must be plainly marked with the pupil's name.
8. No pupil may be absent from School without permission of the Headmaster, except in cases of illness or other emergency. If a pupil has been absent without permission, a note of explanation should be sent as soon as possible to the Headmaster.
9. All pupils should know the addresses of their billeting teachers to whom they should report if difficulties arise.
10. Hosts must be informed when pupils have permission to go home for week-ends.
11. If an air raid alarm is given while pupils are in their billets they must obey their host's instructions immediately.
12. Pupils must remember (a) to keep their bedrooms tidy and clean, (b) to be helpful to their hosts at all times.

R. B. CALDER.

October, 1939. Headmaster.

127 At the beginning of the Second World War children from the Mundella School in Nottingham were evacuated to Stamford. The evacuees were expected to abide by these rules.

KESTEVEN COUNTY COUNCIL --- FIRE GUARD SERVICE.

EA.
8/.01/35.

Street Fire Party Leaders.

Town Hall,
Stamford.

7th February, 1942.

Dear Sir,
                    Training.

        In order that all Fire Guards should be efficient and
capable of dealing with fires, a course of training has been arranged
to commence with a talk on Incendiary Bombs and Fire Fighting hints.
This talk will be repeated on the various dates shown below, and I
shall be obliged if you will warn all Fire Guards in your party. The
dates are fixed so that every person may be able to attend at least
one of them, and all are urged to make every effort to be present at
one of the lectures. A register will be kept.

                    Yours faithfully,

                    E. K. Lawson

                Chief Fire Guard Staff Officer.

Mondays.   February 16th & 23rd, and 2nd March.
Wednesdays.   "   18th & 25th   "   4th   "
All at 8 p.m. at the Stamford Town Hall.

128 As this letter shows, Stamford took its air-raid precautions very seriously.

129 Invitation to the Stand Down dinner of 'E' Coy, 2nd Northants Home Guard.

" E " Coy. 2nd Northants Home Guard.

◼

Your Company is requested at the

STAND DOWN DINNER AND CONCERT

at

MESSRS. BLACKSTONES SOCIAL & RECREATION CLUB

on

SATURDAY, 13TH JANUARY, 1945, AT 19.15 HRS. PROMPT.

Dress : Clean Fatigue.

A first–class Dinner and Entertainment is being provided free of
charge and as the accommodation is limited you must complete and
return the enclosed card not later than Saturday, 30th December,
1944, if you wish to come.

sub-standard tenements in the town; in 1921 official reports show that over 16 per cent of the town's population were living in houses classed as slums. Private enterprise had gone some way to helping the situation when, in 1920, an estate was built in Ryhall and Rutland Roads to house workers from Blackstone's. In the same year, the council began its house-building programme with the first 'council' houses in Melbourne and New Cross Roads. Despite the amount of new building in progress, in April 1928 the Ministry of Health stated that there were too many slum houses in the town. However, it would to be another five years before a slum clearance programme began in earnest.

Following a brief 'reconstruction' boom (1919-21), the bubble of economic prosperity burst, due, in some respects, to foreign competition. In 1924 Hayes and Son closed, to be followed in 1925 by the Pick Motor Company. Industrial strife and unemployment became quite usual throughout the 1920s. Unemployment was high in the Stamford area and those companies that were producing, such as

130 Looking east from St Martin's. In this photograph the second row of houses in Lumby's Terrace can be clearly seen. The maltings are still operating as is the East station. Cuttings Electrical can be seen in Barnack Road.

131 An unusual view of Stamford taken from the old gas works site in Wharf Road.

132 Until 1946 all residents of Browne's Hospital were required to wear this distinctive uniform. After the war, the governors decided to dispense with the practice and to admit women as well as men.

Blackstone's, were forced into short-time working. The General Strike of 1926 had serious repercussions on local industry. It might be argued that, as a result of the local situation, Stamford became the only town in the country where fascists were elected to a town council. In the local elections of 1924, Arnold Leese and Henry Simpson beat the two Labour candidates. Simpson was re-elected in 1927, despite strong Conservative opposition.

The 1930s were difficult years for Stamford with high levels of unemployment and, at one point, there were about one thousand unemployed people in the area. Job-creation schemes were introduced, which included clearing the castle site for a car park. Blackstone's, still one of the town's biggest employers, were again on short-time working

and, in 1936, were taken over by the Gloucestershire firm of Lister. The decade, however, was not without some positive aspects. Other firms had their beginnings in this difficult period. H.G. Twilley, a textile firm, was founded in the 1930s, and Bennett Bros, Manufacturing Confectioners, opened in Scotgate in 1933. The council's house-building programme also continued, and the Fane School was built in Green Lane to meet the needs of the growing number of children now living in the new suburbs.

In 1939 the country was once again at war. With the possible exception of the work undertaken by Lister-Blackstone, there does not appear to have been any vital war work undertaken in Stamford, and possibly because of this the town escaped any serious bombing.

133 Bennett Brothers sweet factory. A wide range of confectionery was produced by this company which began its production in 1933 in Scotgate; later it moved to Halliday's Yard where it remained until the company closed in the 1960s.

134 The east end of High Street before the demolition of the Albert Hall site.

135   The meadows in flood.

136   Occasionally the weather conspires to ruin the mid-Lent Fair, in this instance Bath Row.

Blackstone's was certainly seen as a potential Luftwaffe target, as aerial photographs of the factory, taken on 3 September 1939, reveal! In October 1940 a bomb was dropped on Cornstall Buildings but it failed to explode; the pilot was presumably aiming for Blackstone's, since he went on to machine-gun the factory. Another attempt was made to bomb the factory in June 1942 but, again, they missed their target and hit houses in Rutland Road area; well over 100 houses were damaged with 41 beyond repair. Burghley House escaped damage when bombs fell in the park.

Among the many ingenious ways devised to raise cash for the war effort, the people of Stamford were invited to collect for the town's very own Spitfire. A large board bearing a model plane was erected outside the central cinema and, as the money flowed in, the tiny plane moved higher up the board. The required target of £5,000 was soon reached and the town had its own plane. It carried the town's coat-of-arms and the legend 'Stamford' on the cowling. In 1942, Stamford Warship week raised over £100,000—a significant amount for such a small town. There was, of course, a large transient population, with the influx of servicemen from Wittering and North Luffenham. In the early years of the war children from Nottingham

were evacuated to Stamford as a precautionary measure. A POW camp was built off Empingham Road, mainly for Italian POWs, although for a time it also accommodated German prisoners.

The end of the war in 1945 brought another period of reconstruction. Although there was full employment in the area, the housing shortage was still acute, despite a steady increase in the number of council houses. When the council began building the Drift Road Estate in 1946 it was estimated that there were one thousand people in the town who were in need of housing or rehousing. In the same year 25 pre-fabs were built in King's Road. These were meant as a temporary expedient, but in fact lasted well into the 1970s. In 1948 the old POW camp in Empingham Road was being used as temporary accommodation. In 1954 the Marquess of Exeter opened Stamford's 1,000th council house, and by 1961 a third of Stamford's houses were council-owned.

As people moved out of the town centre into the newly created suburbs, the slum properties were slowly cleared away; and the pubs which had served those communities, such as the *Welland Cottage* (Gas Street), the *Balloon* (Blackfriars Street) and the *Beehive* (Water Street) were closed down. These were replaced by new pubs such as the *Northfields* (1955) and

137 All Saints' Brewery was established in 1820 by William Edwards and was bought by Melbourne's in 1869. In 1974 the brewery was purchased by Samuel Smiths who sub-sequently closed it down. It is now a brewery museum.

138   Following the closure of St Michael's Church in 1963, Christ Church was built in Green Lane to meet the needs of the growing housing estate to the north of the town.

in 1968, the *Danish Invader*. The Church of England finally recognised the population shift and in 1963 St Michael's Church was declared redundant and Christ Church was opened in Green Lane.

The 1960s and '70s showed signs of small-scale industrial growth as some established firms expanded. Cuttings Electrical had already been taken over by Arthur Lyon & Co. Ltd, electrical engineers, and by 1967 had expanded to become Newage Lyon Ltd. In 1987 the company bought Markon Engineering of Oakham and changed their name to Newage International Ltd. A second factory was opened in Ryhall Road in 1997. The Martin Cultivator Co. had moved from Blashfield's old site in Wharf Road to Ryhall Road as early as 1907. Here they continued to produce farm machinery, eventually becoming known as Martin Markham. Another firm that opened in the town was the plastics company Cascelloids, which operated from the site of the Hayes carriage and wagon works in West Street.

In one respect we should perhaps be thankful that the town did not grow as an industrial centre, since the absence of any re-development not only helped to preserve Stamford as a market town, but also as a town which reflects a wide diversity of architectural styles. Stamford's unique qualities and the need to preserve the historic core were underlined in 1967 when the town was designated Britain's first conservation area. With the historic centre of the town now protected, it escaped some of the worst examples of 1960s planning and environmental change. However, this still came too late to preserve the architectural integrity of High Street: the introduction of corporate building design such as that of the then Burtons at no. 5 High Street; and the whole-sale destruction of the Albert Hall site in 1966. Gone was the Albert Hall with its mansard-roofed range of buildings, Deer's shoe shop, Gilbert's greengrocers and the 17th-century *Windmill Inn*. From this redevelopment has risen the Tesco-Pearl Assurance complex, which remains a monument to unsympathetic rebuilding. Elsewhere in the town corporate building has been equally unsympathetic. Where national retailers have preserved the façade of a building they have, more often than not, gutted the interior to meet modern shopping needs.

Stamford's position at the junction of four counties has always been something of an anomaly. The town's failure to achieve county status in the Middle Ages has left it on the periphery, remote from the county town. A Boundary Commission in 1959 proposed that Stamford should be moved out of Lincolnshire into a new county based on Peterborough. All the old arguments for and against moving the town were rehearsed, but to move Stamford out of Lincolnshire would solve nothing. Whatever new authority was created, Stamford would still be on the edge. In the major reconstruction of 1974, Stamford finally lost its borough status and the last remaining privileges of a Chartered Corporation; in its place was a town council with a largely advisory role. The new South Kesteven District Council chose to make its headquarters in Grantham. In practice this means that decisions about Stamford are taken outside the town by people who are remote from the issues. It is true that Stamford has representation on the district council but, in practice, they are few in number compared with the council as a whole. In October 2001 the district council formed an inner 'cabinet' comprising six members of the council. Stamford had no representation in this cabinet, leading to fears that the town's issues may not be fully understood by this decision-making group. This situation may change, but until it does, Stamford has even less say in its own affairs.

However, none of these things has had any impact on Stamford's steady growth. In 1960 the population had reached 11,440; by 1981 it had risen to 16,500, and by 2001 this had increased to about 19,000 inhabitants. But what sort of town is it becoming? At the time of the quincentenary celebrations in 1961, the question was posed, 'Is this a place where people go to school but never stay to work, and where people retire?' The answer to these questions appears to be 'Yes'. Certainly the town's schools are flourishing and it is clear that many families move to the area to take advantage of the opportunities offered by the Endowed Schools. The town has also seen a steady rise in housing development, to the extent that there is now a significant degree of infilling on old commercial sites. The town is clearly seen as a pleasant place in which to retire. Employment opportunity, however, has reduced significantly. With many of the town's larger employers closing, more and more people find they are having to commute to Peterborough and other nearby towns to find work. The town has essentially become a dormitory of Peterborough. In the early 1960s it looked very much as if the town would enter a new phase of its development with the establishment of a university in the town. This hope stayed alive for several years but, in the end, came to nothing.

The quest for more building land is unrelenting and Stamfordians find themselves having to form pressure groups to protect their town from even more development. The plan to build houses on Blackstone's sports ground has been shelved for the moment, but how long before another developer comes along? Under the South Kesteven Local Plan (2001-11) there is a proposal to build 750 new houses between Empingham Road and Tinwell Road. This has met with fierce opposition, those opposed to the scheme rightly pointing out that the size of the development would have a significant impact on the environment as well as increasing pressure on the historic core of the town and on local services. As it is, more and more sites are being sold for building development and housing density increases.

What future can Stamford find for itself? Industrial development on any scale now seems unlikely. In fact, the town's industry has decreased significantly in recent years. Martin Markham, Gibson's foundry, Melbourne's brewery, and Bennett Bros sweet factory, to name but a few, had all gone long before the turn of the 20th century. In 2002 Williamson Cliffe announced their closure after 100 years of brick-making; and in the same year Blackstone's parent company, the German firm of MAN B&W Diesel, decided to close the Stamford operation, bringing to an end an association which had lasted for 165 years. Many local retailers such as Oates & Musson, Bassendines, Parrish & Sons, Dolby Bros, which were once household names in the town, have now long gone to be replaced by national retailers, creating a High Street scene that is replicated in countless other towns throughout the country.

There has been considerable speculation on how Stamford can be kept buoyant and alive given its lack of industrial or commer-

cial base. To some extent, these issues remain unresolved. Developments in recent years suggest that the future lies in encouraging both tourists and light industry to the town. In the 1970s the thought of promoting Stamford as a tourist centre was anathema to many. Yet this now seems one of the few remaining options. Stamford's unspoilt character has already made it attractive to film makers and it was chosen by the BBC as the background to their adaptation of *Middlemarch*. If the future lies in tourism and light industry, then there is an urgent need to resolve the town's traffic problems and to preserve the historic centre of the town. Stamford's streets were never designed to accommodate the size of modern commercial vehicles or the present volume of traffic. Until the opening of the north-south by-pass in 1961, the town had a reputation as a major bottleneck on the A1. The by-pass went some way to reducing the traffic passing

139 For period drama, Stamford has become something of a mecca for film makers. This photograph shows the filming of a scene in St George's Square of a BBC adaptation of *Middlemarch*.

140 The last twenty years have seen a considerable amount of rebuilding, much of it on a disused commercial site. These houses in Water Street were built on the site of a garage.

141 Modern housing on Station Road. These houses have been built on the site of a former timber merchants.

142 In 1963 St Michael's Church became redundant and stood empty for some years. In 1992 it was sold to a developer who divided it into shop and office units. It has been described by Pevsner as 'an unsympathetic use and and appalling conversion'.

through the town, but to resolve the issue completely an east-west by-pass is also needed. A major problem is the sheer size of the lorries trying to negotiate narrow streets and the town bridge; quite often they pass within feet of medieval buildings and we can only guess at the damage they do to the foundations of old buildings. An experimental lorry ban in 2001 resulted in a 19 per cent drop in the number of HGVs using the town. In 2002 South Kesteven District Council are to commission a transport management study. It is to be hoped that this will lead to a greater level of pedestrianisation and a reduction in traffic in the centre of the town.

At the beginning of the 21st century the town is gradually adjusting to its changing circumstances just as it did 400 years earlier; but the future is uncertain. The town has been described as the 'Finest Stone Town in England', but it is in danger of losing this epithet.

Undoubtedly, Stamford has become a pleasant place in which to live. But this is something of a two-edged sword. The increasing demand for housing has already swallowed up many sites and this pattern looks set to continue. In the early part of the 20th century, many slums were cleared and the space they occupied subsequently became car parks, e.g. North Street, Bath Row. The latter half of the 20th century has seen history repeat itself in the sense that many industrial and commercial sites are being cleared to meet the demand for even more housing. It is the character of the town that visitors find attractive, but, if this character is to be preserved, there is a need to ensure that any future building is sympathetic to, and harmonises with, the existing street scene. Alec Clifton-Taylor described the town as having great dignity. It behoves Stamford well to ensure that this dignity is preserved.

A Select Bibliography

Early and Medieval History

Dobson, R.B., *Urban Decline In Late Medieval England*, 1976

Foster, C.W. and Longley, T. (eds.), *The Lincolnshire Domesday and the Lindsey Survey*, 1924

Hartley, J.S. and Rogers, A., *The Religious Foundations of Medieval Stamford*, 1974

Mahany, C., Burchard, A. and Simpson, G., *Excavations in Stamford Lincolnshire 1963-1969*, The Society For Medieval Archaeology Monograph Series, No.9, 1982

Mahany, C., *The Archaeology of Stamford*, 1969

Mahany, C., *St Leonards Priory*, South Lincolnshire Archaeology 1, 1977

Mahany, C., *Stamford—Castle and Town,* South Lincolnshire Archaeology 2, 1978

Owen, D.M., *Church and Society in Medieval Lincolnshire*, 1971

Roffe, D., *Stamford in the Thirteenth Century*, 1994

Rogers, A., *The Medieval Buildings of Stamford*, 1970

Rogers, A. (ed.), *The Making of Stamford*, 1965

Rowley, R., *Norman England*, 1997

Sander, P., *Anglo Saxon Lincolnshire*, 1998

Wild, P.J., *The Romans in the Nene Valley* (*c.*1975)

16th and 17th Centuries

Bowker, Margaret, *The Henrician Reformation*, 1981

Brears, C., *Lincolnshire in the 17th and 18th Centuries*, 1940

Butcher, R., *Survey and Antiquities of the Town of Stamford*, 1646

Davies, C., *Stamford and the Civil War*, 1992

Hodget, Gerald A.J., *Tudor Lincolnshire*, 1975

Holmes, C., *Seventeenth Century Lincolnshire*, 1980

18th and 19th Centuries

Birch, N.C., *Stamford—An Industrial History*, 1972

Curl, J.S., *Georgian Architecture*, 1993

Hodgkinson, E. and Tebbutt, L., *Stamford in 1850*, 1954

Key, M., *Pick of Stamford*, 1994

Reed, M., *The Georgian Triumph 1700-1830*, 1983

Rhodes, J., *Great Northern Branch Lines to Stamford*, 1988

Rogers, A. *et al.*, *A Short History of the Stamford and Rutland Hospital*, 1978

Stamford Survey Group, *Class and Occupation in Stamford in 1851*, 1980

General

Bennett, S., *A History of Lincolnshire*, 1999

Blore, T., *An Account of the Publick Schools, Hospitals and othe Charitable Foundations in the Borough of Stamford*, 1813

Burton, G., *Chronology of Stamford*, 1846

Clifton-Taylor, A., *Stamford*, 1984

Deed, B.L., *A History of Stamford School*, 1954

Glossop, D., *Stamford Fire Fighters 1888-1988*, 1988

Hance, F., *Stamford Theatre and Racecourse*, 1970

Mahany, C.M., *The Archaeology of Stamford*, 1969

Marwick, W.F., *Stamford and the Great War*, 1919

Nevinson, C., *History of Stamford*, 1879

Peck, F., *The Antiquarian Annals of Stanford*, 1729 (republished 1979)

Pevsner, N. and Harris, J., *Lincolnshire*, 1978

Rogers, A., *The Book of Stamford*, 1983

Rogers, A. (ed.), *The Making of Stamford*, 1965

Royal Commission on Historical Monuments, *The Town of Stamford*, 1977

Smith, M., *Stamford Then and Now*, 1992

Smith, M., *The Story of Stamford*, 1994

Smith, M., *Stamford Almshouses*, 1990

Stamford Historian Vols 1-6, 1977-1982

Stitt Dibden, W.G. and Tebbutt, L., *Stamford a Postal History*, 1961

Till, E.C., *A Family Affair, Stamford and the Cecils 1650-1900*, 1990

Wright, N.R., *Lincolnshire Towns and Industry 1700-1914*, 1982

Index

Numbers in **bold** type indicate illustrations